# The Rediscovery of
# Ancient Egypt

PETER A. CLAYTON

# The Rediscovery of Ancient Egypt

ARTISTS AND TRAVELERS IN THE 19TH CENTURY

PORTLAND HOUSE

New York

D. M.

JOHN F. KEANE and LESLIE GREENER

P. A. C.

V. S. L. M.

*Frontispiece* Vivant Denon, frontispiece to the *Description de l'Egypte*, 1809. This is a 'telescopic' view looking south up the Nile, from Alexandria (Pompey's Pillar is on the far right) to Philae in the distance (see the map, p. 56). Features on the west (right) bank include, from near to far: the Sphinx and a pyramid, Dendera, the Ramesseum, Colossi of Memnon and Medinet Habu, Armant and Edfu. On the east bank, in the foreground is the obelisk of Heliopolis; beyond it lie Antaeopolis, Karnak, Luxor and Kom Ombo.

*Passages from Gustave Flaubert's travel notes and from Maxime Du Camp's 'Le Nil, Egypte et Nubie' are reprinted from 'Flaubert in Egypt', translated and edited by Francis Steegmuller (Bodley Head, London, 1972, and Academy, Chicago, 1979), by kind permission of Francis Steegmuller*

This 1990 edition published by Portland House, a division of dilithium Press Ltd., distributed by Crown Publishers, Inc., 225 Park Avenue South, New York, New York 10003

Printed and bound in Spain
ISBN 0-517-01510-2
h g f e d c b a
D.L.TO: 1147-1989

# Contents

# Foreword

In illustrating the rediscovery of ancient Egypt from 1798 until the second half of the 19th century, from the age of the *savant* to the age of the tourist, when the foundations of Egyptology were laid, one is faced with an *embarras de richesses*. The final selection here represents the work of thirty artists, chosen for a wide variety of reasons – because it is important historically, aesthetically pleasing and accurate, interesting archaeologically since a lost monument is represented, or perhaps simply apposite and amusing. There are a number of monuments and sites between Alexandria and Abu Simbel which were continually drawn, sketched or painted, making a choice between them very difficult at times; other interesting monuments seem to have been little visited. There are also sites which were hardly known at this period and which have therefore had to be left out altogether, such as the superb temples at Abydos and Deir el Bahari.

Some artists, too, have had to be left out – because they were less interested in topographical views than in details of monuments and inscriptions, or because their original light sketches are too faint for reproduction. Notable among them are the Britons James Burton, Edward Dodwell and Henry Parke; the French Jean-Baptiste Adanson, Jean Nicolas Huyot and Nestor L'Hôte, and the Swede Baltzar Cronstrand. Some have left a vast quantity of material that needs to be worked through with a sympathetic eye with a view to even partial publication. L'Hôte has been fortunate in having received the attention of Madame Vandier D'Abbadie; selections from the work of Sir John Gardner Wilkinson are shortly to be made available via microfiche; and it is hoped that Leslie Tillett's research on the Robert Hay manuscripts and diary will also find publication.

Among all the artists working in Egypt in our period one stands head and shoulders above the rest, both for the number of sites and monuments he recorded and for his interesting presentation – David Roberts. His are the only works that have survived in any great number to the present day, due largely to his prodigious output of sketches and finished drawings; and he is also well known through the lithographs from his *Egypt and Nubia*.

In writing a book such as this an author benefits from many kindnesses, from the quality of conversations on the subject and the facilities so readily granted for research with original material. Thanks are due to many people, and to none more so that Mr Rodney Searight, whose magnificent collection and wide knowledge of artists in the Middle East are so freely and pleasantly made available to all who enquire of him. I am also indebted to Mr Michael Wolfe-Barry (great-grandson of Sir Charles Barry), with whom, together with his wife Margaret, a most pleasant cruise was spent on the Nile in March 1980; to Miss Helen Guiterman and to Mr Frank Bicknell (great-grandson of David Roberts); to Miss Helen Murray of the Griffith Institute, Oxford, for her kind responses to queries and her help with archive material; to the staff of the Drawings Collection, Royal Institute of British Architects Library, London, for their never failing and courteous help with the Barry material; and also to the staff of the Library of the Society of Antiquaries of London, whence many of the early engravings were obtained. Last, but by no means least, an acknowledgment is due to my wife for her patience in having lived with so many of the 'ghosts' in this book, especially Belzoni's, for so many years.

P.A.C.

# The Rediscovery of Ancient Egypt

## *The early days*

The first tourist to visit Egypt and to leave an account was Herodotus of Halicarnassus, in the mid-5th century BC. Called the 'Father of History' by the Roman statesman Cicero, Herodotus was researching the material for Book II of his *History* on the spot. To do so he travelled extensively in Egypt and as far south as Aswan. His account is fascinating reading – a mixture of fact and fable, wonderment, scepticism and gullibility all tumbled together in varying degrees. At times he quite forcibly expresses his own opinion about what he has been told, invariably by members of the Egyptian priesthood. He cannot, for instance, believe the explanation given for the annual flooding of the Nile: 'It is, that the inundation of the Nile is caused by the melting of snows. Now, as the Nile flows out of Libya, through Ethiopia, into Egypt, how is it possible that it can be formed of melted snow, running, as it does, from the hottest region of the world into cooler countries?' His reasoning appears quite sound, but in this case the explanation was basically correct. In other areas he accepts the most outlandish tales and repeats them. Curiously, as our knowledge of certain areas of archaeology has increased, a number of his often disregarded comments have been proved to be correct. Herodotus' account, which is still of great interest and value today, was to be used as a source by several other Classical writers four centuries after him. Diodorus Siculus and Strabo leant heavily on his *History* while also adding new material in writings based on

Victorious Gaul rediscovering ancient Egypt: bronze medal commemorating the French conquest in 1798 and the *Description de l'Egypte*, by Barre, 1826 (see p. 27)

their own observations. In Classical times Egypt was a lure for tourists, as the numerous Greek and Latin graffiti still extant on many of the monuments show.

The Greeks and Romans were not the first, however, to show an 'archaeological' concern for Egypt's past. During the Saite period (26th Dynasty, 664–525 BC), a hundred years before Herodotus' visit, there had been a great resurgence of interest by Egyptians in their own antiquity. Research was carried out into earlier history, stories, etc.; art forms looked back to the Middle and Old Kingdoms, especially in sculpture, and restorations were carried out on some monuments of those periods. The wooden coffin of Mykerinus, builder in c. 2540 BC of the third pyramid at Giza, was restored, and possibly also his stone sarcophagus [13].

After the battle of Actium in 31 BC Octavian, as he was then known, became master of Egypt and the last queen, Cleopatra VII, committed suicide. Although Egypt nominally became part of the Roman Empire when Octavian became Augustus in 27 BC, it retained a curious status. It was governed from Rome and garrisoned by legions (III *Augusta* and XXII *Deiotariana*), but was looked upon as part of the emperor's private estate. Such was its importance as one of the granaries of Rome that Augustus decreed that no member of the imperial family or of the Senate might visit the country without his express permission. During his reign, which lasted until AD 14, Augustus began the process of moving monuments within Egypt, and also of removing them, that was to reach its peak in the 19th century.

Most of the obelisks had been erected at the two great religious centres, Heliopolis and Thebes (modern Luxor and its environs). Some single obelisks were erected, but most were in pairs flanking the entrance to a temple, standing before the pylons [39]. A number were moved from their ancient sites to Alexandria and re-erected there, while others continued on over the Mediterranean to Rome. Pliny devotes a chapter of his *Natural History* (XXXVI, 14) to obelisks, giving details of many of them and of the pharaohs who erected them. The Egyptians had cut the obelisks as single pieces of granite from the quarries at Aswan [63] and then floated them on barges down the Nile to their intended site, where they were finished and erected. Details of the barges are represented in a relief in Queen Hatshepsut's temple at Deir el Bahari (c. 1490 BC), where two obelisks to be dedicated at Karnak are seen in transit. Pliny tells us that 'the most difficult enterprise of all, was the carriage of these obelisks by sea to Rome, in vessels which excited the greatest admiration. Indeed, the late Emperor Augustus consecrated the one which brought over the first obelisk, as a lasting memorial of this marvellous undertaking, in the docks at Puteoli; but it was destroyed by fire.' A subsequent ship that brought another obelisk, at Caligula's orders, was preserved as a wonder of construction for several years, and then taken to Ostia where it was sunk and used as the basis for work in the new harbour.

The obelisk, to the ancient Egyptian, was a symbol of the *benben*, the sacred stone of the sun god at Heliopolis (see p. 60). Many were erected specifically to Amun-Ra and their inscriptions invariably invoke the god or record royal victories. The hieroglyphs could not be properly read in Roman times and Pliny incorrectly asserts that two of the obelisks re-erected in Rome, in the Circus Maximus (now in Piazza del Popolo) and the Campus Martius (now in Piazza Montecitorio), bore inscriptions 'which interpret the operations of

Nature according to the philosophy of the Egyptians'. The example in the Campus Martius was used as the *gnomon* or marker of an enormous sundial and Augustus' inscription, added to the base, told that he had presented it to the Sun: '*Soli donum dedit*' – an appropriate continuation, in a way, of its original dedication.

The first obelisk erected in Rome, by Augustus, is the one that now stands in the Piazza del Popolo. In 10 BC it was set up in the Circus Maximus on the *spina*, the low wall down the centre of the course. Besides its dedication to the sun god, Sol, it was also a monument to the conquest of Egypt by Octavian/Augustus. From that first beginning more and more obelisks were shipped to Rome. Today thirteen still stand in the city, erected on their present sites at various dates: in Piazza S. Pietro (1586), on the Esquiline (1587), in front of S. Giovanni in Laterano (1588), in Piazza del Popolo (1589), Piazza Navona (1649), Piazza della Minerva (1667), Piazza della Rotonda (1711), Piazza del Quirinale (1786), in front of S. Trinità dei Monti (1789), in Piazza Montecitorio (1792), at the Villa Caelimontana (1817), on the Monte Pincio (1822), and finally in the Viale delle Terme (1925). Seven of them have pharaonic inscriptions, two have inscriptions by Roman emperors, one a pseudo-Egyptian text, and the rest are uninscribed. The sheer physical bulk of the obelisks, let alone the numbers involved, shows how very interested the Roman emperors were in these objects. Other Egyptian items were also collected and are referred to by Classical authors, but the obelisk was the paramount symbol and had to be possessed.

As Rome fell into decay so did the obelisks. Many of them broke as they toppled over, and they were lost in the general dereliction of the city. Then in medieval times interest in ancient Egypt revived, infecting the scholarly and the pseudo-learned alike as they read all sorts of fantastic tales and accounts into their interpretation of the hieroglyphs. Pre-eminent amongst such scholars was the Jesuit priest Athanasius Kircher (1602–80). He tried hard to read the names on the Roman obelisks but, like so many of the students of the time, was entirely misled by accepting that the signs were purely symbolic. His work on Coptic and his four large tomes entitled *Oedipus aegypticus* (1652–54) did much to arouse a scholarly interest in ancient Egypt and were the most important in this respect until Napoleon's expedition a hundred and fifty years later.

In Christian Europe Egypt was intriguing not only for its mystery but for its biblical associations, most evident in the stories of Moses and Joseph. (The pyramids were often referred to as the 'granaries of Joseph'.) There were some intrepid travellers, virtually all pilgrims on their way to the Christian sites in the Holy Land, who saw a little of Egypt, but most of their observations were confined to the delta and the area around the Giza pyramids. Few ventured further south, having no need to for their pilgrimage. Not least of their problems was the fact that Egypt, since the Arab invasions of the 7th century, was no longer a Christian country and they were hardly welcome. The tradition of Christianity in Egypt, founded by St Mark and nurtured by St Anthony and the other Desert Fathers, which evolved into the Coptic Church with all its internal squabbles over doctrine, had to give way to the greater force of Islam. Typical of the hardship of a Christian in an Islamic country in the Middle Ages is the tale in the late 9th century of Bernard the Wise and his two companions who landed at Alexandria from Rome. Gold was extorted from them before they were allowed ashore; their papers were utterly useless when they finally made their way to 'Babylonia' (originally a Roman fortress, later the Christian quarter in the southern suburbs of Cairo), where they were imprisoned for six days before having the wit to bribe their way out. The letters they were then given did not save them from having to pay a few more silver coins each time they were required to produce their documents. The party eventually reached their goal, Jerusalem, overland. It is little wonder in view of such experiences, and the fact that Christians were subject to a poll tax, that scarcely anyone ventured into Egypt for the next six hundred years.

The first traveller to leave a fairly full account in the Middle Ages was the Dominican Friar Felix Fabri of Ulm in Germany. In 1480 he decided to go on a pilgrimage to the Holy Places and travelled by land and sea to Jerusalem, returning via Sinai and Egypt in 1483. His *Evagortium in Terram Sanctam* ranks with the *Canterbury Tales* in the way in which the reader is caught up in the pilgrimage. The journey across the desert to Sinai, to St Catharine's Monastery and the site of the Burning Bush, was full of terror and wonder; it took twenty-six days, which only the strongest and fittest could hope to survive. They then passed on to Cairo to see the Virgin's Well and the crypt where the Holy Family sheltered in the church of St Sergius in Old Cairo. They saw the pyramids and Fabri noticed, as they took ship at Alexandria for Europe, 'a very remarkable column, all of one stone, yet of wonderful height and width. On the four sides were carved men and animals and birds from the top to the bottom; and no one now knows what these figures signify.' Four hundred years later that obelisk [VI] also left Alexandria, to end up in Central Park, New York.

With the Renaissance and the increasing stability of the Middle East, more travellers frequented the southern shores of the Mediterranean. Venetians put into Alexandria with their great galleys, returning to the port whence they had stolen the holy relics of St Mark to make their own city a place of pilgrimage on the Adriatic. The published accounts were invariably wildly garbled, often because the writers imagined more than they actually saw. The drawings they made of the Sphinx and the pyramids are as amusing as they are inaccurate. The first scientific treatise on the pyramids was written by John Greaves in his *Pyramidographia* (1646). His approach was an astronomical one (he held the Chair at Oxford) and he was well versed in the writings of the Classical and Islamic astronomers. Once again, he was ahead of his time and his approach was not to be emulated until the French expedition in 1798. More travellers journeyed south, but although they saw the obelisks peeping out of the rubbish heaps at Karnak and Luxor they failed to equate the site with Homer's 'hundred-gated Thebes'. The vivacity of the accounts published makes them enjoyable if not informative reading, as Leslie Greener has pointed out in *The Discovery of Egypt*.

In 16th-century Rome interest was stirring in the obelisks that were beginning to come to light. The Vatican obelisk was the only one still standing. Augustus had placed it in the Forum Julia in Alexandria, but Caligula had demolished the Forum and ordered the obelisk to be brought to Rome, where it was erected in AD 37. Like the bronze equestrian statue of Marcus Aurelius on the Capitol, the Vatican obelisk probably escaped being toppled as a pagan symbol because of its alleged Christian association. St Peter, it was said, had met his death along with thousands of other Christians in the Vatican Circus and the obelisk was regarded as a silent last witness to the martyrdom of the Fisherman. Several of the early 15th-century popes had considered moving the obelisk to the piazza in front of St Peter's great basilica but due to various complications, not least financial constraints, had done nothing.

It was left to Sixtus V (Pope from 1585 to 1590) to achieve what others had failed to do; he might well be dubbed 'the Obelisk Pope'. The obelisk, properly consecrated and 'de-paganized', was seen as a most suitable monument to the Christian Church and teachings. Sixtus, in the five years of his short pontificate, managed to re-erect four obelisks and was also interested, before death took him, in re-erecting three others: those now in the Piazza Navona, at the Trinità dei Monti, and on the Quirinal. On a bronze medal he is shown in splendid vestments on the obverse, while the reverse shows the four obelisks surrounded by the legend 'CRVCI FELICIUS CONSECRATA'. The obelisks are, from left to right, those in the Piazza del Popolo, at S. Giovanni in Laterano, Piazza S. Pietro, and the Esquiline.

Bronze medal of Pope Sixtus V, by Peretti. On the reverse are the four obelisks that he had re-erected in Rome by Domenico Fontana

Sixtus appointed Domenico Fontana as the engineer to undertake the enterprise of first lowering the uninscribed obelisk in the Vatican Circus and then erecting it in the Piazza S. Pietro. It was a daunting task at best, made more so by having to lower and lift simultaneously a single shaft of stone 25.37 metres (83 feet) tall and weighing about 326 tons, liable to fracture at any awkward strain. Fontana constructed a huge wooden cradle to encase the obelisk and aid its lifting but, when it was raised, it was found to be resting on four bronze crabs, of which two were loose but the other two, each weighing some 150 kilograms (330 pounds), were dovetailed to both obelisk and pedestal, and nothing could proceed until the stone had been chipped away to free them. (The bronze crabs, sacred to the sun god Sol, were a feature of the ancient Roman re-erection of obelisks.) The obelisk was placed on its cradle on 28 April 1586, lowered, dragged to the piazza and re-erected, and formally purified, dedicated and crowned with a cross on 26 September. The feat aroused great popular excitement, and honours were heaped upon Fontana.

Sixtus now became anxious that Fontana continue with the re-erection of the Esquiline obelisk, one of a pair that had stood before the mausoleum of Augustus. This was much smaller than the Vatican example, and Fontana was able to raise it in August 1587. Sixtus next turned to the obelisk said to be in the Circus Maximus. This had been brought from the temple of Amun at Thebes (Karnak [XI]) to Alexandria by Constantine the Great and, after his death, transported to Rome by his son Constantius in 357. There it was erected in the centre of the *spina* (the obelisk of Augustus being moved to the east side of the Circus). It was now found, at a great depth, broken into three pieces. Fontana was called upon once more and it was re-erected before S. Giovanni in Laterano in August 1588. It is the tallest obelisk extant (32.18 metres, or 106 feet) and weighs around 455 tons. Sixtus's fourth and last obelisk was the one that had been the first to come from Egypt. Its fragments were discovered in the Circus Maximus, where its base with the inscription of Augustus had been found during the reign of the previous pope. With Fontana again the engineer in charge, it was set up in March 1589 in the Piazza del Popolo.

Obelisks continued to be re-erected, mainly on papal instructions, until the last, which was the Dogali obelisk, discovered in Rome in 1883. Originally

11

Pietro della Valle, *Examining mummies at Dahshur,* from *Petri della Valle . . . Reiss-Beschreibung,* 1674, the first illustrated German edition of his work

erected in 1887 in front of the old Termini railway station, it became a traffic obstruction and was removed to its present site in 1925. It commemorates Ramesses II in its inscription and, on its pedestal, the five hundred Italian soldiers who fell at Dogali, Abyssinia, in 1887.

In the 17th and early 18th centuries many more travellers went to Egypt out of curiosity and interest rather than as part of a pilgrimage or merchant venture. Notable amongst them was Pietro della Valle (1586–1632), who described the Giza pyramids and surrounding monuments, and sought mummies and other objects. Two of the mummies he collected at Dahshur were in the Dresden Museum until their destruction in the Second World War. A number of the travellers were still men of the Church: Father Claude Sicard (1677–1726), a French Jesuit missionary, went to Cairo in 1707 and made many journeys into the 'interior'. He discovered and identified Thebes, which so many had passed over before him, and he was the first European traveller since antiquity known to have gone as far as Aswan, where he described the temples of Kom Ombo, Elephantine and Philae. Although he was principally concerned with trying to convert the Copts he had specific orders from Philippe d'Orléans to take notice of and draw the monuments he saw as he made his journeys to the great Coptic monasteries and communities. By 1722, four years before his death from plague, he had located many of the major monuments: 20 of the principal pyramids, 24 complete temples and over 50 decorated tombs. Another Frenchman, Paul Lucas (1664–1737), travelled in the Near East and collected antiquities. He is particularly noted for his exploration of the extensive underground galleries at Saqqara containing mummies of sacred ibis, where much new work has been undertaken in recent years by the Egypt Exploration

Friderik Ludvig Norden, *The Sphinx and pyramids of Giza*, from his *Travels*, 1757

Society. Thomas Greenhill, an English surgeon, published an engraving of the Saqqara catacombs in 1705 in his book ΝΕΚΡΟΚΗΔΕΙΑ, *or the Art of Embalming*, but never visited Egypt. A more thorough examination of sites in Middle and Upper Egypt was made by Dr N. Granger of Dijon (d. 1733), who discovered the superbly decorated 19th Dynasty temple of Seti I at Abydos. It was deeply buried in the sand, and although Dr Granger managed to get in by a window, 'after having dug it around', his discovery was to remain relatively unnoticed until the temple was cleared of its sandy burden in 1859 by Auguste Mariette.

In 1743–45 the Rev. Richard Pococke (1704–65), later to be Bishop of Ossory and Meath, published two folio volumes entitled *A Description of the East, and some other countries*. He was an inveterate traveller and his detailed descriptions, comments and measurements are invaluable for a number of monuments that disappeared between his visit to Egypt in 1737–38 and the French and German records not a hundred years later. As the French were to be, he was much impressed by the zodiac ceiling in the Ptolemaic temple of Dendera [32], and he was rather more accurate than they when he surmised that it was 'by one of the best Greek Sculptors': the French believed it to be of high antiquity because of its zodiacal representations. Travelling at the same time as Pococke was the Danish naval captain Friderik Ludvig Norden (1708–42). He had been sent there expressly by Christian VI of Denmark to produce a full and accurate account of the country. His *Travels* was first published in 1751 and ran to several editions, as well as English and German translations, because of its able text and drawings. The last of the great 18th-century travellers in Egypt was James Bruce (1730–94) of Kinnaird, Scotland.

He set out in July 1768 and travelled south into Abyssinia, returning to Britain in 1773. He carried out a number of explorations and the tomb of Ramesses III in the Valley of the Kings, which he cleared, is still known as Bruce's Tomb (or the Harper's Tomb, from the representation of harpists in it).

Such, broadly, was the situation and knowledge about Egypt towards the end of the 18th century. The days of exaggerated travellers' tales were coming to an end. Egypt had long been the source of all the best that was mysterious; not least was the fascination of the mummies and their alleged medical properties. Sir Thomas Browne in his *Hydriotaphia, or Urn Burial* (1658), inspired by the discovery of a cemetery of burial urns, noted how 'mumiya' was used, crushed and taken in liquid, as a universal panacea. Mummies continued to command a high price both as curiosities and as a source of remedies. With the coming of the French expedition the door was to be opened for the rediscovery of Egypt in a proper and scientific manner. Mummies began to be robbed for their papyri rather than broken up for their pharmaceutical properties.

# The French conquest, the British landing and the aftermath

Shortly after dawn on 19 May 1798 a French fleet set sail from the port of Toulon. This vast latter-day Armada was carrying over 34,000 men plus animals, guns and munitions and was heading for the open sea under sealed orders. The flagship was the impressive 120-gun, triple-decker, *L'Orient*, captained by Louis Casabianca. On board he had two very important passengers, Admiral of the Fleet Brueys and Napoleon Bonaparte. Although few aboard knew it at the time, their objective was Egypt and their aim was to 'rescue' the country from her Turkish overlords, the Ottoman Empire, ruled by the Sultan from Constantinople. The Turks had been viewed with suspicion and, indeed, alarm for several centuries by Europeans. Turkish brutality to captured Christians was notorious, and had been one of the main reasons for the great confrontation between Christianity and Islam at the naval battle of Lepanto in 1571.

In Europe in the 1790s the nations watched France and her rising general, Bonaparte, with distrust. After the completion of his highly successful Italian campaign in 1797 the Directory had much the same feelings about him. He was young, a victorious and self-opinionated leader, and, as Christopher Herold has aptly commented, 'it is dangerous to have unemployed heroes loitering about'. Rome had been in a similar situation with Julius Caesar when he returned victorious with legions at his back, and Napoleon was a great admirer of both Caesar and his great-nephew Octavian/Augustus. England viewed the threat of Bonaparte with dismay since he had been appointed commander of the 'Army of England', but fortunately he considered that at the time he lacked the necessary resources to carry out a successful invasion. French attention turned towards the East – to the Ottoman Empire racked by internal troubles and thus a ready prey for any designs by Russia or England. Talleyrand, the newly appointed French Foreign Minister, realized that France needed more colonies and trade; what better way to pursue the war against England than to menace her overland route to India, via Egypt? France would gain a colony at the expense of the Ottoman Empire, busily engaged elsewhere, and would also solve the problem of the young general who was fast becoming an embarrassment. So the decision was taken and almost two hundred ships put to sea on that May morning, less than three months after the plans had been approved by the Directory at the end of February.

In addition to the warlike cargo of men and munitions on board the fleet there was a Commission on the Sciences and Arts consisting of 167 scientists and technicians, including many eminent scholars representing virtually all the sciences of the day, under the leadership of Baron Dominique Vivant Denon. The sixteen cartographers and surveyors among them were to play a very important part in the birth of Egyptology. It is amazing to think that only some forty people in all knew where their travels were to take them.

The fleet's passage lay past Malta, which capitulated after only two days. The treasure of the Knights, valued at around seven million gold francs, was taken on board the *L'Orient*. Alexandria was sighted on 1 July and disembarkation of the troops began the same day off Marabut beach, about 13 kilometres (8 miles) west of the city. To have sailed directly into one of the two harbours at Alexandria would have been hazardous without detailed charts, and could also have been highly dangerous militarily. The assault began early on 2 July and the next morning the city surrendered to Napoleon. Because of his need to recover from wounds, Major-General Jean-Baptiste Kléber was made military governor of Alexandria. On the afternoon of 7 July the fleet was brought round to a better anchorage in the shallow bay of Aboukir, some 24 kilometres (15 miles) east of Alexandria. The army then set off under their commander, Louis Charles Antoine Desaix, across the desert towards Cairo. All the way they were harassed by Bedouin, who were highly mobile compared to the wretched French soldiers stifling in their tight and heavy European uniforms and manoeuvring heavy equipment. One daydreaming officer was killed a mere hundred paces from the advance guard. The soldiers suffered from the sun and from lack of water and bread, and a number of them died not at enemy hands but from heatstroke or suicide.

At about 2 p.m. on 21 July the French army began to order itself in front of the Mameluke lines, drawn up some way off. Behind the Mamelukes, in the far distance, they could see the strong outlines of the Giza pyramids; many of them wondered what they were. A couple of engagements had already been fought with the troops of the Turkish commander, Murad Bey. While the Mameluke approach was all dash and light cavalry, the French relied stolidly on their formation in squares and their superior European discipline. Napoleon now ordered the usual disposition of the troops: hollow squares, six ranks deep, baggage and what little cavalry there was inside them and artillery at the corners. He records that he addressed his men before the engagement, appealing to their sense of history: '*Soldats! du haut de ces pyramides quarante siècles vous contemplent!*' (He was remarkably accurate in his guess, and it was a guess since no one knew the age of the pyramids at this period: the Great Pyramid was at the time some 43 centuries old.) On a number of medals struck to commemorate the 'Battle of the Pyramids' Napoleon is variously seen gesturing dramatically in the shadow of the pyramids – whereas Giza was in

Two versions of Napoleon's famous address to his troops before the Battle of the Pyramids: a bronze uniface striking of a medal, and a bronze medal by A. Bovy

Louis François Lejeune, *The Battle of the Pyramids*, 1806. In this detail Napoleon appears on horseback at the far right, his troops pushing the Mamelukes into the Nile. In the distance, beyond an infantry square, are the pyramids of Giza

fact about two hours' march away. Curiously, the dates given on the medals, 23 and 25 July, are also inaccurate.

The French, some 25,000 men, had both a numerical and a tactical superiority. The carnage was terrible as the Mamelukes time and again hurled themselves against the squares, firing from the saddle or swinging their scimitars. The battle lasted about two hours, then the Mamelukes broke and fled. Many of those who managed to get clear of the field were either cut down in the pursuit or drowned as they tried to cross the Nile, at that time of the year in flood. The French soldiers busied themselves stripping the bodies: there were rich pickings to be had – apart from his weapons and fine clothes of silk every Mameluke carried vast amounts of wealth about his person, and it was nothing for two or three hundred gold pieces to be found on the corpses, especially on many of those fished from the Nile, whose bodies, as soon as they were despoiled, were thrown back to continue downstream.

On 22 July a deputation was sent from Cairo to Napoleon at Giza, and two days later he entered the city and sent a despatch to the Directory detailing the events. 'It would be difficult', he concluded, 'to find a richer land and a more wretched, ignorant, and brutish people.'

Napoleon was safely in his headquarters in Cairo, but his advantage was soon to be lost. Out in the Mediterranean Nelson with a British fleet had been seeking the French. He was aware that they had left Toulon, and had made an informed guess as to their destination. After a protracted game of blind man's buff, he heard that the French had definitely sailed for Alexandria and altered course due south. As the British neared the Egyptian coast Captain Thomas Hood of the *Zealous* signalled that he had sighted the French at anchor. Nelson (who all the while was suffering from a raging toothache) ordered dinner and the attack, in that order. He had already worked out various battle plans. The following day – he remarked to his officers assembled on board his flagship – would see him either in the House of Lords or in Westminster Abbey.

Aboukir Bay is a magnificent long curve of shallow, shelving beach. No reliable charts of it existed, so the French Admiral Brueys had anchored his thirteen men o'war in line astern about 2 kilometres ($1\frac{1}{2}$ miles) offshore, with some 45-metre (50-yard) intervals between them. At the ends of the line he anchored his four frigates. In the early afternoon of 1 August working parties were ashore foraging, digging wells, or fetching provisions from Alexandria and Rosetta, and many of them ignored the frantic signals from *L'Orient* to return aboard ship. Brueys thought that he had some time in hand, as the normal course would have been for the British to send a light vessel forward to reconnoitre, but Nelson had other ideas: his fleet of fourteen 78-gunners and the brig *Mutine* sailed straight for the French, helped along by the late afternoon north breeze that occurs on this coast. Brueys had reasoned that his landward side was protected by the shallowness of the waters of the bay, and most of his fleet had withdrawn their landward guns. Had the ships been closer together, they could have presented an invincible wall of cannon fire against Nelson, but in the early evening the first British ships passed between the westernmost of the French ships and the shore, missing the shoals and coming along their landward side, broadsiding as they went. Nelson, on the *Vanguard*, attacked and was wounded by a piece of shrapnel, which cut his head above his good right eye, temporarily blinding him.

The Battle of the Nile: at sunset, British ships are in position between the French ships and the shore. Reverse of the bronze commemorative medal by C. H. Küchler for Alexander Davison

17

Louis Casabianca and his son aboard the doomed *L'Orient*. Bronze plaque by L. Patriarche, 1910

By 8 o'clock on board the *L'Orient* Admiral Brueys was dead and his captain, Louis Casabianca, wounded in the head; but it was Casabianca's thirteen-year-old midshipman son who achieved immortality among the heroes that night, dying with his father when the flagship blew up, sending the treasure of the Knights of Malta hurtling into the night sky above the bay. It was of him that Felicia Dorothea Hemans wrote the emotive, evocative and instantly popular poem that begins with those well-known words,

> The boy stood on the burning deck,
> Whence all but he had fled . . .

On the morning of 2 August the battle ended. Only four of the French ships, which had been anchored at the distant end of the bay, escaped. So many prisoners were taken that they had to be returned to the shore and put on parole not to fight against the British. They could fight as much as they liked against the Mamelukes! Denon had witnessed the entire battle from the tower of a convent near Rosetta. On the morning of 1 August the French had been masters of Egypt; in one day, he reflected, the navy had thrown away the army's gains and lost an empire. Napoleon and the French were cut off in Egypt.

England was jubilant when the news reached home. Nelson achieved the House of Lords, being created Viscount Nelson of the Nile and Burnham Thorpe (his birthplace in Norfolk). Alexander Davison, his prize agent, had bronze, gilt, silver and gold medals struck at his own expense by Matthew Boulton at the Birmingham Mint to be awarded to all who had taken part in the battle, according to their rank. On the reverse is a view of the British fleet sailing into action at Aboukir with the sun setting on the horizon, surrounded by a legend which reads, 'ALMIGHTY GOD HAS BLESSED HIS MAJESTY'S ARMS' – the opening words of Nelson's despatch to George III written, with a curious foreknowledge, when he was still under medical care, before the *L'Orient* had blown up and the outcome was sure. Many other medals and 'favours' were readily available on the streets of London and the cartoonist James Gillray published a number of satirical prints with Egyptian overtones relating to the battle and the French defeat.

Back in Egypt Desaix was busily pursuing the fleeing remnants of the Mameluke forces south into Upper Egypt. With him went Vivant Denon (1747–1825), who was to be one of the founding fathers of Egyptology. Through his connection with the *salon* of Joséphine de Beauharnais Denon had met Napoleon, and was appointed head of the *savants* on the expedition. A person of an enquiring nature, he was well liked – as he had been throughout his earlier, chequered, scholarly and diplomatic career – and a good artist. The drawings which he and other members of the party made were intended for a vast and definitive *Description de l'Egypte*. By the time that was published, in 1809, it had been pre-empted by Denon's own account of his travels, *Voyage dans la Basse et la Haute Egypte*, which was first published in 1802 and was instantly popular, running to several editions and being translated into English and German. Denon is a delightful character, forever making objective comments about what he saw while at the same time appreciating the humour of the awful scrapes he got himself into from time to time. He was great friends with his commander: Desaix (1768–1800) had an amused tolerance for the scholar, loved jokes, was noted for his bad dress, would as soon wrap himself in his cloak under a cannon as seek a comfortable bed, and was adored by his men. Even Napoleon recognized, in his memoirs, that Desaix 'was intended by nature for a great general'.

Denon's *Voyage*, when translated into English in 1803, was again an immediate success. He was well served by his translator, Arthur Aikin, who made some judicious comments on Denon and the French expedition in the 'Advertisement by the Translator':

> It is presumed that an account by an eye-witness of the romantic but unprovoked invasion of Egypt by General Bonaparte, will not be uninteresting to the British Public . . . The work contains an agreeable mixture of incident and description . . . of the campaigns in Upper Egypt, he [Denon] is as yet the only historian: in this view, therefore, his narrative is of peculiar value.

There is also a very modern ring about the cost of the English edition:

> Notwithstanding the liberal allowance of plates, it has been found expedient, for fear of too much enhancing the price of this edition (the French original of which sells in London for twenty-one guineas [£22.10p] to leave out a few which are contained in the original.

Louis Charles Antoine Desaix de Veygoux, after a drawing by General Belliard

The French edition consisted of two elephant folio volumes, one of text and one of plates, whereas the English edition was two quarto volumes with integrated plates.

Denon realized that he was the 'spare' in the military establishment pursuing the Mamelukes, but remarks,

> If a fondness for antiquities has frequently made me a soldier, on the other hand, the kindness of the soldiers, in aiding me in my researches, has often made antiquaries out of them.

His scholarly interest often overcame his military awareness, and he would have to be rescued, almost by the scruff of his neck, by a small patrol sent to bring him up with the main column. He met other difficulties as well:

> There are some unlucky moments, when everything one does is followed by danger or accident. As I returned from this journey back to Benesuef, the general charged me with carrying an order to the head of the column; I gallop on to execute it; when a soldier who was marching out of his rank turning suddenly to the left as I was passing to the right, presents his bayonet against me, and before I could avoid it, I was unhorsed by the blow, whilst he at the same time was thrown down. 'There is one savant less' said he while falling, (for with them every one who was not a soldier was a *savant*); but some piastres which I had in my pocket received the point of the bayonet, and I escaped with only a torn coat.

Beni Suef seemed to be an unfortunate place for Denon – later that day his horse ran away with him and he only got back to the camp after nightfall. He missed his way and when his horse suddenly stopped he urged him on, jumping a trench he did not know was there and ending up against a palisade, not being able to move either forward or back.

> At this time the sentinel challenged me, I did not hear him, and he fired: I called out in French; he asked what business I had there, chid me, and turned me out; and thus the aukward *savant* was bayonetted, fired at, chid, and sent home like a truant school-boy.

Vivant Denon, *Denon sketching the ruins of Hieraconpolis*, from his *Voyage*, 1802

Denon often makes asides to the reader, as:

Here the pitiless reader, sitting quietly at his table with his map before him, will say to the poor, hungry, harassed traveller, exposed to all the trouble of war: 'I see no account of Aphroditopolis, Crocodilopolis, Ptolemais – what is become of all these towns? What had you to do there, if you could not give any account of them? Had you not a horse to carry you, an army to protect you, and an interpreter to answer all your questions – and have I not relied upon you to give me some information on all these subjects?' But, kind reader, please to recollect, that we are surrounded with Arabs and Mamelukes, and that, in all probability, I should be made prisoner, pillaged, and very likely killed, if I had thought proper to venture only a hundred paces from the column to fetch some of the bricks of Aphroditopolis.

Due to the constant change of direction of the Mamelukes Desaix's force often had to retrace its path, so Denon had the opportunity of visiting several sites more than once. He was especially pleased when this happened at Edfu [57] and Dendera. At times he is very philosophical about when he can make his drawings and plans, and at the Ramesseum at Thebes he comments,

It would have taken some time and examination to have made out the plan of this temple, but the cavalry were galloping on, and I was obliged to follow them closely, not to be stopped for ever in my researches.

Now and then he slips into the sketches a figure of himself or one of his staff, shown busily drawing. At Hieraconpolis he, his servants and horse take precedence over the ruins he is sketching against the sunset. Often their camp was simply in the shade of a rock or some palm trees. Once he depicts himself relaxed at 'our Head Quarters in the Tombs near Nagadi':

This gloomy habitation was a great relief to us in the desert, and preserved us from the heat of the most scorching sun. The scene is taken when the peasants of Nagadi were bringing in to us the Meccans, who, after their defeat, had turned robbers, and desolated the country; whom, therefore the Nagadians killed whenever they met with them. The time represented is midnight, the Arabs of Nagadi are coming in with their prisoners, lighted by a kind of torch, which is much employed in Egypt during night marches; on the other side are our coptic stewards and interpreters, and in the centre, General Beliard, his etat-major and myself; the whole is a faithful picture of our situation at the time.

Denon had a kindly eye both for the soldiers with whom he was travelling (who seem to have regarded all the *savants* with a benign tolerance) and for the local populace who, in the main, were simple and much overawed by the European troops.

Napoleon was personally very interested in Egyptian antiquities and collected some objects for himself. He had founded an 'Institut d'Egypte' in Cairo immediately on his arrival, and its members were expected to investigate all matters concerning Egypt. Denon often strayed from his antiquarian studies to examine the fauna, being especially intrigued by the crocodiles found basking on the sandbanks.

Vivant Denon, *Bivouac at Nagadi*, from his *Voyage*, 1802. Denon is seated in the foreground. The central figure on the mat is General Belliard

Napoleon visiting the
headquarters of the recently
founded Institut d'Egypte in
Cairo, 1798, from the *Description
de l'Egypte*

While at Keneh I had to regret the death of a crocodile, which some peasants having
surprised asleep, had bound and brought alive to the officer who commanded during
the absence of General Belliard: the animal being yet young, and fettered by an iron
circle between the shoulders and belly, could not be very formidable . . .

He speculates on all aspects of the beast, on the possibilities of taking it to
France for study, etc., and it is tempting to see in this passage the germ of the
idea for Gillray's caricature of the Institut attempting to tame and ride
crocodiles [V]. Denon proudly recounts how,

On his return to Cairo, Bonaparte examined attentively all the drawings that I had
brought back, and [was] satisfied that the object of my mission had been
accomplished . . .

Denon had accompanied the pursuit of the Mamelukes backwards and
forwards along the Nile and must be allowed his little piece of self-
congratulation:

We collected a great number of camels, I say *we*, because by degrees one identifies
one's self with those that one lives with, and I was a party concerned in every event

that happened to the division of Desaix, and more particularly to the twenty-first demi-brigade. I partook of its dangers, its successes, its misfortunes, and I persuaded myself that I came in for some share of its glory.

Of his work he wrote,

> For the last nine months my thoughts had been wholly occupied in the collection of interesting objects, so that I was entirely ignorant of my situation and future resources: I had shrunk from no dangers in satisfying my curiosity, and the apprehension of being obliged to quit Upper Egypt, without having seen all that was best worthy of remark there, would have induced me, without reluctance, to go through still greater perils. Circumstances arising from the unsettled state of the country, and the necessary subservience of my own particular designs to the military operations, had in many instances prevented me from taking more than a hasty glimpse of objects that would have amply recompensed a longer stay; but even if my researches shall have no other effect than abridging the future labours of those who may succeed me in a time of greater tranquillity, I shall rejoice that my zeal has been thus far at least serviceable to the arts.

His output, especially when one considers the conditions under which his work was done, was nothing less than prodigious.

Denon finally proceeded to Alexandria, ready to try to return to France. This was not easy, since the British had blockaded the Egyptian coast since the victory of the Nile, intercepting virtually every French ship that tried to run in or out of Alexandria, but when he arrived,

> the first things that struck my attention were two of our frigates ready for sea, lying at single anchor off the new port; not a single English cruiser was in sight, and I began to believe in prodigies.

The following day, 22 August 1799, at one in the morning he and his companions were summoned and found Napoleon waiting to travel with them. They managed to run the blockade by slipping along the North African coast,

> along the arid shores of the ancient Cyrene . . . well convinced that we were under the guidance of no mean star, we indulged our joy in security.

At last they made a safe arrival at the port of Fréjus, having dodged an English squadron whose guns they could hear in the thick fog that enveloped and protected them.

The first Kléber knew that he was now Commander-in-Chief in Egypt was after Napoleon's departure. He received a despatch in which Napoleon declared, 'I will arrive in Paris, I will chase out this gang of lawyers who mock us and who are incapable of governing the Republic and I will consolidate this magnificent colony.' Kléber felt that he had been abandoned and very forcefully expressed his opinion in despatches to France. Fortunately for his military career they were intercepted by British ships. In France, a lead 'jetton' or token was issued glorifying Napoleon. Around a Republican-style portrait he is saluted as 'Liberator of Egypt'; the reverse shows a figure of Hermes or Mercury flying before curiously steep-sided pyramids, with the legend, 'The hero restored to his country'. Gillray's cartoon of the episode, on the other hand, is bitingly satirical and speaks of the 'Deserter of the Army of Egypt' as revealed by Kléber's intercepted despatches. Another cartoon showed an amusingly caricatured line-up of French officers before the army medical

BUONAPARTE leaving EGYPT.

For an illustration of the above, see the Intercepted Letters from the Republican General Kléber, to the French Directory respecting the Courage, Honor, & Patriotism, of – the Deserter of the Army of Egypt.

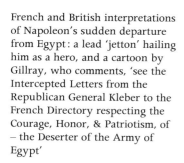

French and British interpretations of Napoleon's sudden departure from Egypt: a lead 'jetton' hailing him as a hero, and a cartoon by Gillray, who comments, 'see the Intercepted Letters from the Republican General Kleber to the French Directory respecting the Courage, Honor, & Patriotism, of – the Deserter of the Army of Egypt'

officer; a crocodile (traditional symbol of chemists) is suspended from the ceiling on tricolor ribbons and, swathed in the background, stand two mummies labelled 'Napoleon' and 'Kléber'.

Left alone in Egypt Kléber had to suppress a revolt in Cairo and fight a battle at Heliopolis against Turkish forces in the autumn of 1799. Then, on the afternoon of 14 June 1800, tragedy struck. Kléber was walking with an aide in the Citadel above Cairo when an Arab approached him, apparently begging for a favour or baksheesh. As they drew near the Arab brought a knife out from behind his back and stabbed Kléber, who fell dying. By a strange quirk of fate, on the same day and within the same hour that afternoon Desaix, Kléber's old second-in-command, was killed in Italy on the battlefield of Marengo, which he had turned into a last-minute French victory. (Both men were commemorated by medals. On that of Desaix his Egyptian associations were recalled by the head of the Sphinx and Cleopatra's Needle.)

With Kléber's death the Egyptian command fell to General Jacques Abdullah Menou, a convert to Islam and a poor soldier – both facts which the English satirists, especially Gillray, took full advantage of in their cartoons.

In the early spring of 1801, nearly three years after Nelson's victory at Aboukir, a combined naval and military force under the command of Admiral Lord Keith arrived at Alexandria. The French had been very busy in Egypt, despite the British blockade, and the time had come for their complacent attitude to be shaken. The British army, commanded by Lieutenant-General Sir Ralph Abercromby, landed on 8 March. As with most events of national importance and interest, there were a number of commemorative medals and engravings produced. The pyramids of Giza appeared on the reverse of one medal and were to continue to be extensively featured on most items that referred to Egypt. The battle of Alexandria was fought on 21 March and several British regiments gained notable battle honours, especially the Gloucesters and the Black Watch (42nd Foot), but Abercromby was mortally wounded and died on board the *Foudroyant* on 28 March. The medallion struck to mourn his death featured the Giza pyramids yet again, monuments that he never saw.

Major-General Lord Hutchinson took command of the victorious army and it fell to him to implement the terms of the Treaty of Alexandria that was drawn up. In its initial draft the treaty had included the stipulation that all the notes gathered by the French *savants* should be forfeit. They rejoined that if their notes were to go into captivity, so would they. A compromise was reached: under Article XVI of the Treaty, the French kept their notes but had to hand over all antiquities found by them and to relinquish all rights to any seized at sea by the naval blockade. An inventory of fifteen antiquities in the possession of the French at Alexandria, certified by J. B. J. Fourier, Secretary to the Institut d'Egypt, and handed over to Colonel Sir Tomkyns Hilgrove Turner, was found amongst the latter's papers and is now in the British Library (BL Add. MS 46839F).

The chief prize was item 8 in Fourier's inventory – the Rosetta Stone, a distinctively shaped piece of inscribed basalt, found by an officer of engineers, P. F. X. Bouchard, at Fort Julien on the Rosetta mouth of the Nile in 1799. He had recognized its possible importance and reported it to General Menou, who

Aspects of the British 'delivery' of Egypt: *above left*, medal commemorating the British landing; *far right*, sketches by Sir Robert Ker Porter of General Menou on a camel, Lord Keith aboard the *Foudroyant*, the landing, and the Sphinx and pyramids; and *above right*, medal celebrating the Treaty of Alexandria

promptly took it under his personal 'protection'. (Many of the French officers acquired some fine pieces in this manner.) Turner wrote an interesting account of the Stone's acquisition, which was read before the Society of Antiquaries of London, in their rooms in Somerset House in the Strand, on 8 June 1810 (*Archaeologia*, XVI, 1812). General Menou had at first insisted that the Stone was his private property, but eventually it was collected from his house in a 'devil cart' by a detachment of artillerymen. Before it left Alexandria, the French were allowed to ink the Stone's surface to take copies, using it as a printing block, and also to take casts. Turner then accompanied it back to England in the appropriately named frigate the *Egyptienne*. On 11 March 1802 it was deposited in the Library of the Antiquaries, and later in the year it was transferred to the British Museum, to which, along with the other trophies of war, it had been presented by George III. More casts of it were made and many scholars came to study it; fortunately scholarship transcended the boundaries of war. The Rosetta Stone held the key to the future of Egyptology (see pp. 46–47).

Although the French nominally left Egypt in 1801 their influence in the country continued to benefit it for many years, especially in banking and law (Egyptian law still reflects the Napoleonic Code in many of its aspects). In 1831 the ties were strengthened when Mohammed Ali, Viceroy of the Ottoman Sultan, presented to France one of the obelisks from Luxor [39], which was set up in Paris in the Place de la Concorde amidst great popular rejoicings on 25 October 1836. It was a Frenchman, Champollion, who was *the* founding father of Egyptology (see p. 47), and several famous French scholars were to follow in his footsteps. Auguste Mariette (1821–81) founded the Egyptian Antiquities Service and was instrumental in setting up the old Cairo Museum (in a house in Bulaq, a suburb of the city), which was the first national museum in the Near East. He excavated widely in Egypt, discovering fresh monuments, clearing others, working at thirty-five different sites in all. Not only was he a major Egyptologist, but he also wrote, with C. du Locle, the libretto of *Aida*, Verdi's great opera which had its premiere in Cairo in 1871. When Mariette died his remains were buried in a replica of an Old Kingdom stone sarcophagus which now rests in the garden of the present Cairo Museum. Mariette's successor as director was another great Frenchman, Sir Gaston Maspero (1846–1916), and the line of French directors of the Antiquities Service continued into the 20th century.

Bronze medal commemorating the erection of the obelisk from Luxor (see p. 109) in the Place de la Concorde, Paris, on 25 October 1836. The inscription gives details of the obelisk's size and weight and of its re-erection

# Travellers, scholars, artists and collectors

After his return to France Denon was appointed Director of the Central
Museum of Arts in 1802 and, in 1804, Director-General of Museums, a post
which he held until 1815. He was responsible for numerous commemorative
medals, several of which related to the Egyptian campaigns; all, without
exception, ignored the naval defeat at Aboukir. The concept and designs of
some of the medals are particularly pleasing. One shows a most unusual three-
quarter-front face portrait of Napoleon with a wreath of lotus flowers, symbol
of ancient Egypt, above his head. On the reverse he is seen as a Roman general
crowned by Victory, riding in a chariot drawn by two richly caparisoned
camels towards Cleopatra's Needle and Pompey's Pillar in Alexandria [VI, IV].
The Roman allusion appears again on another medal, but subtly disguised: the
obverse is a Neoclassical artist's rendering of a pharaoh's head [p. 72], but the
reverse shows a crocodile chained to a palm tree – a conceit referring to a
Roman coin issued at Nemausus (Nîmes) in southern France under Augustus,
commemorating his victory at Actium when he became master of Egypt.
(Sailors from the Roman fleet had been settled at Nemausus, hence the choice
of subject.) One of the most attractive designs is a small medalet that
commemorates Denon himself. On the reverse is a view of the Colossi of
Memnon [41, 42], the northern one of which was said to moan at dawn and
dusk, until silenced by repairs carried out during the reign of Septimius
Severus; charmingly, the legend on the medallion records: 'ELLES PARLERONT
TOUJOURS POUR LUI' – the allusion being that the monuments of ancient Egypt
always spoke to Denon. He certainly brought them to life. Egyptologists today
owe him a great debt for his meticulous drawings of monuments now lost.

The first edition of the monumental *Description de l'Egypte* was published
in 1809. On the engraved and highly ornamental frontispiece (see p. 2), framed
within an Egyptian portico emblazoned with military trophies and names, is a
complicated montage of the principal monuments and a number of objects. (The
'Altar of the Four Divinities', as the red granite sculptured block at the foot of
the foremost obelisk was called, was subsequently collected by Belzoni and is
now in the British Museum. Belzoni's name and the date 1817 are carved on its
top surface.) Much of the text was edited by Edmé François Jomard
(1777–1862), an engineer with Denon's party in Egypt; he also made some
drawings for the *Description* [19, 22], but his chief contribution was six
volumes of the commentaries. Other illustrations were engraved after drawings
by Balzac, Cécile, Chabrol and Dutertre. Baron René Edouard Devilliers du
Terrage (1780–1855), a civil engineer among the *savants*, was particularly noted
for his reconstruction drawings, usually made in conjunction with J. Jollois [30,
53, 60]. The publisher was C. L. F. Panckoucke.

A fine large bronze medal was struck to commemorate the *Description*
showing, on the obverse, France in the guise of a Roman general 'rediscovering'
Egypt as he unveils an Egyptian queen recumbent on a crocodile. On the
legionary standard appears the Gallic cockerel with, in the background, the
three pyramids of Giza and the façade of the temple at Dendera [p. 7]. The
reverse [p. 29] carries an involved design of Egyptian gods and goddesses, with
a scarab at the top and an ankh sign of life at the bottom. The hieroglyphs
give the names of the divinities correctly, an unusual attention to detail.

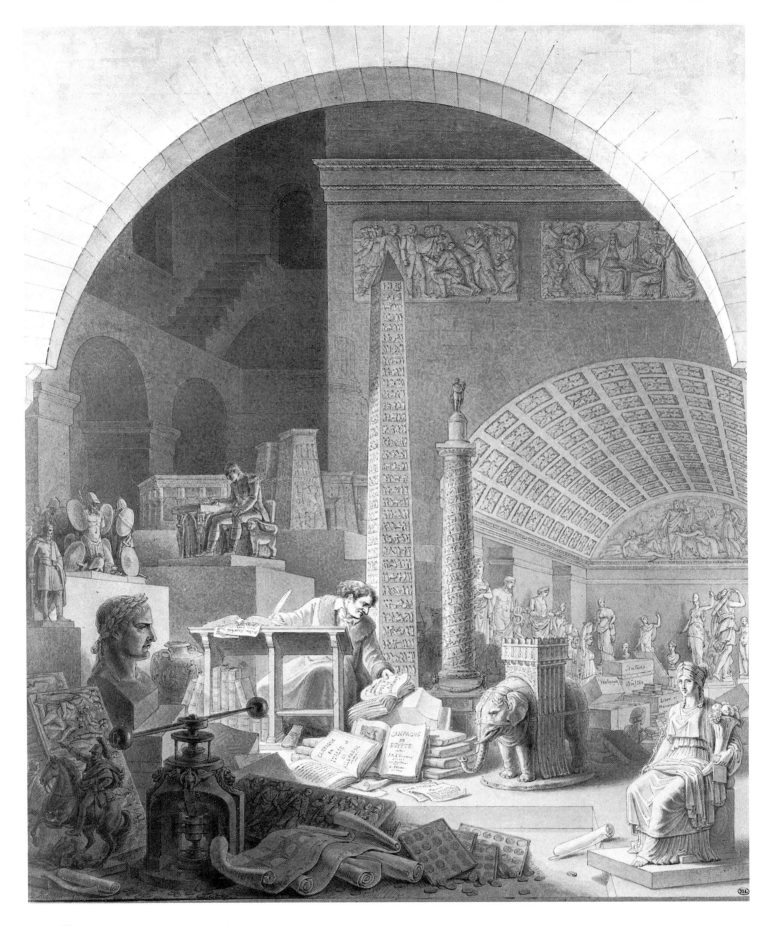

28

◁ *Allegorical Portrait of Baron Denon* by Zix. The scholar is shown in an imaginary Neoclassical setting which alludes to his post as Director of Museums, surrounded by evidence of his interest in Greece, Rome and Egypt. Above left are models of Philae; in the foreground are a coining press and medals

*Right* Reverse of the bronze medal celebrating Louis XVIII's furtherance of the publication of the *Description de l'Egypte*, by J. J. Barre, 1826. (For the obverse, see p. 7)

(a,b) Bronze medal commemorating the conquest of Egypt in 1798, issued under Denon's direction, with obverse by J. Jouannin and reverse by L. Brenet

(c) Reverse of a bronze medal commemorating the conquest of Upper Egypt, 1798, by A. Galle. (For the obverse, see p. 71)

(d) Denon's model: a Roman coin of Colonia Nemausus, on which the chained crocodile refers to the capture of Egypt by Octavian in 30 BC

(e,f) Bronze medallet commemorating Denon himself, bearing his portrait and the Colossi of Memnon

a

c

e

b

d

f

The Hon. Charles Leonard Irby, painted by J.-B. Borely in oriental dress, with the Nile and the island of Philae in the background

The names of James Mangles and Charles Irby, carved in May 1817 at Dendera on the edge of the roof above the portico of the temple (see Ill. 31)

With the handing back of Egypt to the Sultan of Turkey by the British a gate had been opened to the Near East. The Napoleonic wars in Europe restricted travellers on the normal grand tour to Italy, and many extended their itineraries to include Egypt. A typical explanation is that given by Irby and Mangles in the Preface to their *Travels in Egypt and Nubia* (1823):

On the 14th of August, 1816, the Hon. Charles Leonard Irby and James Mangles, Commanders in the Royal Navy, left England with the intention of making a tour on the continent. This journey they were led to extend far beyond the original design. Curiosity at first, and an increasing admiration of antiquities as they advanced, carried them at length through several parts of the Levant, which have been little visited by modern travellers, and gave them more than four years of continued employment.

They left their names inscribed on the roof of the temple at Dendera in May 1817, shortly before they joined Belzoni in opening the temple at Abu Simbel (see p. 174).

Amongst the travellers in Egypt in the early 19th century one stands, quite literally, head and shoulders above the others: Giovanni Battista Belzoni (1778–1823). The artist Benjamin Robert Haydon wrote in his journal in 1821 that 'Belzoni is a glorious instance of what singleness of aim and energy of intention will accomplish. He was a man with no single pretension to calculate on attaching his name to Egypt, but by his indomitable energy he had attached Egypt to his name for ever . . .' Born in Padua, Belzoni left the city at the time of the French invasion in 1798, wandered in Europe for several years and went to England in 1803. He was of immense size, about 2 metres (more than 6 feet 6) in height, and earned a living at first on the music hall stage appearing as the 'Patagonian Sampson'. The highlight of his act was, almost by a premonition, the Human Pyramid, when he wore an iron harness upon which ten or twelve people could perch and be carried around the stage. He tired of the touring life and decided to go, with his wife Sarah and their Irish servant lad James Curtin, to seek his fortune in Constantinople. On the way there in 1815 on Malta he met an agent of Mohammed Ali, who was seeking European engineers. Belzoni had studied hydraulics as a young man and his small party was soon in Egypt. Vested interests at court, however, made quite certain that his improved water wheel was not accepted, and the three of them were left stranded.

At this point Fate took a hand. Henry Salt (1780–1827), the recently appointed Consul General of Great Britain in Egypt, had been urged by Sir Joseph Banks to use his position to collect antiquities for the British Museum. Salt, himself trained as an artist [42] and interested in the monuments, gave Belzoni his first Egyptological commission in which his mechanical knowledge and great strength were to play an important part. He was instructed to remove from the Ramesseum at Thebes the huge granite bust known as the 'Younger Memnon'. This he proceeded to do [XVIII] against considerable opposition from the local people, who were concerned not with the monument but with how much they could make from it – a factor he had to reckon with more than once in the next three years.

R. H. Norman, *Sig. Belzoni the Patagonian Sampson as he appeared at Sadlers Wells Theatre on Easter Monday 1803 Carrying Eleven Persons the Iron Apparatus Weighing 127 lbs*

I David Roberts, *Approach of the Simoon, Desert of Gizeh, or A Recollection of the Desert on the Approach of the Simoon*, from *Egypt and Nubia*, 1846–50

'The dust-cloud grows and comes straight at us . . . It is reddish brown and pale red; now we are in the midst of it. A caravan passes us coming the other way; the men, swathed in *kufiyehs* [headcloths] (the women are thickly veiled) lean forward on the necks of their dromedaries; they pass very close to us, no one speaks; it is like a meeting of ghosts amid clouds . . .'
Gustave Flaubert, travel notes, 18 May 1850

*This splendid composition shows how Roberts, who was basically very accurate, could become carried away by the effect of his subject. The juxtaposition of the Sphinx, pyramid and sun is incorrect, as the Sphinx, the embodiment of Ra-Herakhti, the rising sun, faces directly east. Holman Hunt was indignant, but Charles Dickens, to whom Roberts presented the original painting from which this lithograph was made, was delighted and considered it 'a poetical conception'.*

II Edwin Long, *The Gods and their Makers*, 1878

*This was Long's third Egyptian picture, painted four years after his visit to Egypt and Syria in 1874. It is typical of his work, reflecting the vast amount of research he put into minute details (the stool in the foreground is copied from an actual specimen preserved in the British Museum). The* atelier *is concerned with manufacturing and providing largely funerary furnishings. On the ground at the left are* ushabtis, *mummiform figures to be buried with the dead to work in the next world; canopic jars for the deceased's internal organs line a high shelf in the room beyond. A patient cat acts as model for a sculpture that must be associated with the cat-headed goddess Bast. Sketches on the rear wall are taken from ostraka (limestone sherds) and humorous papyri.*

III Edwin Long, *Anno Domini* or *The Flight into Egypt*, 1883

*Long's fifth Egyptian subject is a vast canvas that subtly makes a dramatic contrast between the two 'Great Mothers', setting the simplicity of the Holy Family in their flight to sanctuary against a religious procession bearing a statue of the goddess Isis nursing her son Horus. While the small details are as usual meticulously rendered, Long was not too concerned with geographical accuracy. In the background looms the great Ptolemaic temple of Horus at Edfu (with two seated colossi added before the pylons; compare Ill. 58) and beyond in the haze are the pyramids of Giza. The two sites are actually nearly 800 kilometres (some 480 miles) apart.*

I

III

II

IV

"L'Insurrection de l'Institut Amphibie". ___ The Pursuit of Knowledge

Etched by J.ᵗ Gillray, from the Original Intercepted Drawing.

V

VI ▷

VIII

◁ VII

'We passed near Pompey's pillar . . . If the shaft on this column, separating it from the pedestal and the capital, once belonged to an ancient edifice, it is an evidence of its magnificence, and of the skill with which it was executed. It ought therefore to be said, that what is called Pompey's pillar, is a fine column, and not a fine monument; and that a column is not a monument.'

Vivant Denon, *Travels*, 1803

IV *Vivant Denon, Measuring the column of Pompey, Alexandria,* July 1798

*Pompey's Pillar has nothing to do with Pompey: it received its name from the medieval belief that it marked Pompey's tomb. It is a red granite pillar with an overall height of 27 metres (88 feet) that was set up in AD 292 by the Roman prefect Posidius in honour of the emperor Diocletian.*

*Gillray was the foremost of the British satirical caricaturists who had a field day at the expense of the French after Nelson's decisive victory at Aboukir (the Nile) on 1 August 1798. Here Gillray ridicules the new French* Institut *set up in Cairo under the direction of Vivant Denon to study all aspects of the flora, fauna and monuments of Egypt.*

V James Gillray, 'L'Insurrection de l'Institut Amphibie' – The Pursuit of Knowledge, 12 March 1799

'We came afterwards to the obelisk, named Cleopatra's needle; another obelisk thrown down at its side, indicated that both of them formerly decorated one of the entrances of the palace of the Ptolemies, the ruins of which are still to be seen at some distance from thence . . . They might be conveyed to France without difficulty, and would there become a trophy of conquest, and a very characteristic one, as they are in themselves a monument, and as the hieroglyphs with which they are covered render them preferable to Pompey's pillar, which is merely a column . . .'

Vivant Denon, *Travels*, 1803

VI *Vivant Denon, View of 'Cleopatra's Obelisk', Alexandria,* July 1978

*Denon's suggestion was not followed: neither obelisk went to Paris, and they are now separated by the Atlantic Ocean (see pp. 58–59).*

*At the inundation the rising waters of the Nile flooded across the cultivated land to the edge of the desert plateau upon which the pyramids rose. They are here seen from the south-east.*

VII David Roberts, The Pyramids of Geizeeh from the Nile, from Egypt and Nubia, 1846–50

'This view is taken from a high rocky ground, above a fountain, where there are some sycamore and palm-trees, and looking nearly due north-west towards the Great Pyramid, that of Cheops, on the right . . . When were these pyramids erected? Wilkinson had powerfully advocated their very high antiquity, and carries them back to the twenty-second century before the Christian era. But Wathen . . . has arrived at the conclusion that they are not earlier than the tenth century before Christ.'

William Brockedon, note to David Roberts, *Egypt and Nubia*, 1855–56 ed.

VIII David Roberts, Pyramids of Geizeeh, from Egypt and Nubia, 1846–50

*The three pyramids in fact date from the 26th century BC. Roberts' view also shows one of the flat-topped mastabas (see p. 70), and the Sphinx.*

Giovanni Belzoni in Turkish dress, after a drawing by Maxim Gauci, 1820

Bronze medal commemorating Belzoni's opening of the pyramid of Chephren at Giza, 1818, by T. I. Wells after William Brockedon

With the mission completed Belzoni travelled up the Nile to visit other sites, drawing many, excavating at others. His record of finds and discoveries is outstanding: he opened the great temple of Ramesses II at Abu Simbel on 1 August 1817 [XXVIII, XXIX], and discovered several tombs in the Valley of the Kings, including the finest of all, that of Seti I, on 18 October 1817 [46]. On the west bank of the Nile, excavating behind the Colossi of Memnon, he found several statues and one fine granite seated figure of Amenophis III. He carved his name on its base, beside the left foot – as so many of his contemporaries, for instance his rival Bernardino Drovetti, were doing. At Karnak he found a colossal head of an 18th Dynasty pharaoh, Tuthmosis III or Amenophis III, together with its arm, itself 3 metres (nearly 10 feet) in length. Many other smaller or less important statues were also retrieved. His next major coup was to find the entrance to the second pyramid of Giza (that of Chephren), which since antiquity had been thought to be a solid mass [9–11]. Friends in Britain commissioned a bronze medal to commemorate this feat. Although the artist, William Brockedon, got a very good likeness of Belzoni on the obverse he failed completely with the pyramid on the reverse, obviously because he had no illustration to go by: he shows not Chephren's but the Great Pyramid of Cheops, with its distinctive truncated top.

When Belzoni left Egypt in 1819 he first returned to his native Padua, where he was presented with a substantial solid gold medal listing his exploits and illustrating two statues of the lioness-headed goddess Sekhmet that he had presented to the city. Back in London again, he arranged for the publication of his *Narrative of the Operations and Recent Discoveries within the Pyramids, Temples, Tombs and Excavations, in Egypt and Nubia*, by John Murray in October 1820, and also for an exhibition of his finds, casts and drawings. This opened in the Egyptian Hall, Piccadilly, on 1 May 1821 and drew huge crowds. He was lionized by London society, but grew weary of it and decided to set out on another expedition, this time to find the source of the river Niger. Just before he left he presented the huge granite lid of the sarcophagus of Ramesses III to the Fitzwilliam Museum, Cambridge. At Benin he contracted dysentery, and on 3 December 1823 he died at Gato near Benin, where he was buried beneath an arasma tree. His widow, Sarah, refused to believe at first that he was dead. They had been through so much together in Egypt that it seemed impossible. But on 15 June 1825 she wrote to her friend Jane Porter, the novelist, 'I have at last received the fatal ring – in my heart hope did linger till the fatal ring arrived.' (It was Giovanni's masonic signet ring, brought to her from Africa eighteen months after his death; she subsequently used it to seal her own letters.) She commissioned a memorial engraving showing a portrait of Belzoni surrounded by all his major discoveries and lived on, mainly in poverty but faithful to his memory, until 1870. Howard Carter, the discoverer of the tomb of Tutankhamun, regarded Belzoni's account of his experiences in Egypt as 'one of the most fascinating books in the whole of Egyptian literature', and

Memorial engraving commissioned by Sarah Belzoni showing her husband and his major discoveries, set against the landscape of Thebes. The objects include a pharaoh's head and arm (in the British Museum), the 'Younger Memnon' (far right; see Pl. XVIII), the sarcophagus of Seti I, and the Philae obelisk

43

*Above* Henry Salt, after a portrait by J. J. Halls

*Above right* Charles Barry, by John Hayter, 1838

of Belzoni himself he wrote, 'This was the first occasion on which excavations on a large scale had ever been made in The Valley [of the Kings], and we must give Belzoni full credit for the manner in which they were carried out' – a fine epitaph on the 'Padua Giant' turned Egyptologist.

With Belzoni's help, Henry Salt had accumulated a fine collection of antiquities, both for the British Museum and for himself. After lengthy negotiations, it was bought by the niggardly Trustees of the Museum for a mere £2,000, less than it had cost him in overheads for excavation and removal. The Trustees refused the finest piece, the alabaster sarcophagus of Seti I, and the architect Sir John Soane paid £2,000 for it alone. Belzoni did not get a penny of the money. Salt's second collection, formed in 1819–24, which included the lower half of the sarcophagus of Ramesses III, was bought by the King of France for £10,000, and is now in the Louvre. The third collection, formed in 1824–27, was sold after Salt's death at Sotheby's, many of the items being bought by the British Museum.

Among those who arrived in Egypt in 1818, two were to leave important records: the young English architect Charles Barry, and the even younger Frenchman, L. M. A. Linant de Bellefonds. Barry (1795–1860) was in Athens, about to return home from a Grand Tour that had taken him through Europe to Turkey and Greece, when he met Mr D. Baillie, who much admired his work, and offered him a salary of £200 a year plus expenses to go to Egypt and draw. He travelled extensively in Egypt, going as far south as the Rock of Abusir in

Nubia, where he carved his name and the date, 1819. (In 1873 Amelia Edwards clambered up the rock; her party found Belzoni's name, but 'looked in vain' for other famous signatures.) Barry's diaries, written in ink in a very small and neat hand, contain detailed notes on the monuments he visited, made plans of, and drew in pencil [e.g. 5, 39]. On Wednesday 13 January 1819, sailing downstream, he records,

> we fell in with the Consul's [Henry Salt's] Flotilla towing up the river on the left bank. We put to shore and remained the whole day with the Consul, Mr Bankes and his party. We breakfasted together on the low flat sandy bank. Mr Salt showed me the whole of the sketches that have been made since leaving Philae. They were all in pencil and very numerous. They are the work of himself, Mr Beechey (whom he calls his Secretary) and a French artist named Linant [de Bellefonds]. I looked over Mr Bankes' drawings, which, on account of their great number, he kept in a basket. They principally relate to detail such as hieroglyphs, ornaments etc. and are executed by himself and an Italian doctor in his employ [Dr Alessandro Ricci, who also drew for Belzoni]. All the drawings made by Mr Salt and his employee, belong to Mr Bankes.

Everyone who went on the Nile took his sketchbook, since at that period it was considered a proper accomplishment for a traveller to be able to record his experiences with the brush as well as the pen. Barry was the first English architect to visit Egypt and leave a record. He was knighted in 1852 and is better known for his architectural work, notably the design, with Pugin, of the Palace of Westminster (the Houses of Parliament). He shared with David Roberts the distinction of having an Art-Union of London medal struck commemorating him. Curiously he has another connection with Egyptology, for he rebuilt Highclere, the family home of the 5th Earl of Carnarvon, discoverer with Howard Carter of Tutankhamun's tomb.

Louis Maurice Adolphe Linant de Bellefonds (1799–1883), whom Barry met on the Nile, had journeyed widely in the Near East before arriving in Egypt in 1818. There he met the wealthy antiquarian William John Bankes (d. 1855), and joined his party, going south as far as Dongola in the Sudan (ancient Nubia). In the next six years he travelled extensively there, drawing numerous monuments, of which many have now been totally destroyed, badly damaged, or removed from their original sites to escape flooding by Lake Nasser [66, XXX]. Linant de Bellefonds completely identified himself with Egypt, living in the country for the rest of his long life. A geographer and engineer, he became Minister of Public Works, and in 1873 was given the title of Pasha in recognition of his activities on behalf of Egypt. Many contemporary diaries and accounts mention him.

Another traveller who was to leave his mark went to Egypt in 1821 at the age of twenty-three and remained there for the next twelve years. John Gardner Wilkinson (1797–1875) made two journeys to the Second Cataract [69], and carried out numerous excavations in the Theban area. (Several of the tombs in the Valley of the Kings still bear his painted number allocated to them near the entrance.) In his meticulous application to his work he was often the first to suggest identifications later postulated by others. He identified the site of the Labyrinth at Hawara long before Lepsius, for instance, and recorded Beni Hasan and Amarna before Champollion or Rosellini. Wilkinson returned to England in 1833, and used his observations as the basis for his three magisterial

William John Bankes in oriental dress, by Maxim Gauci, c. 1820

Sir John Gardner Wilkinson in oriental dress, by Henry Wyndham Phillips, 1844

The Rosetta Stone

volumes, *The Manners and Customs of the Ancient Egyptians*, published in 1837. In 1839 he was knighted. He revisited Egypt in 1842, 1848–49, and 1855. Wilkinson is regarded as the founder of British Egyptology, being a pioneer in the decipherment of hieroglyphs, the first to recognize several royal names, and first to make detailed surveys of all the major sites in Egypt, single-handed, and to make a complete plan of Thebes. His contribution was enormous, and honours were heaped upon him by British and foreign learned societies.

Between the arrival of Wilkinson in 1821 and that of Frederick Catherwood in 1823 a momentous event had taken place in Egyptian studies: Champollion had published his *Lettre à M. Dacier*, which was the turning point in the study and decipherment of hieroglyphs. Before then, no-one could understand the inscriptions which so generously covered many of the monuments and obelisks; now it was apparent that antiquities and papyri would be able to speak with their own voices. Champollion's *Lettre* stands at the end of a story that had begun with the discovery of the Rosetta Stone (pp. 25–26). The Stone is inscribed in three scripts and two languages; from top to bottom, they are Egyptian hieroglyphs, demotic (a cursive version of the pictorial hieroglyphs), and Greek. The Greek text was quickly and easily read to show that the inscription recorded a decree of the priests of Memphis in favour of Ptolemy V, recognizing all the good works he had done. It was dated to 196 BC. The first studies of the demotic script were made by the Frenchman Baron Antoine Isaac Silvestre de Sacy (1758–1838) and the Swede Johan David Åkerblad (1763–1819). Silvestre de Sacy was the first to recognize and translate three words of demotic, one of them being 'Ptolemy'; Åkerblad proceeded to associate all the proper names found in the Greek with their demotic equivalents and to identify the words for 'temples' and 'Greeks'. Both, however, failed to recognize that the script was not totally alphabetic, and it was left to the English physician and physicist Dr Thomas Young (1773–1829) to realize that ancient Egyptian consisted mainly of phonetic signs. Young also deciphered the names of Berenice and Cleopatra, using for the latter the text on the obelisk recovered from Philae in 1817 by Belzoni for its discoverer, Bankes (it is now in the park of Bankes's house, at Kingston Lacy in Dorset).

A young scholar, a pupil of Silvestre de Sacy at the Collège de France in Paris, Jean François Champollion (1790–1832), had been fascinated by the problem of hieroglyphs since childhood and he prepared himself for the task of decipherment by learning many of the languages of the ancient Near East, and especially Coptic. He was only sixteen years old when he read a paper before the Grenoble Academy presenting Coptic as the language of ancient Egypt. In his *Lettre* of 1822 Champollion corrected the list of alphabetical hieroglyphic characters that Young had drawn up and then went on, until his death in 1832, to decipher correctly the names and titles of the Roman emperors as they appeared in hieroglyphs, to make a classified list of the hieroglyphic signs, and to formulate a system of grammar. He travelled widely in Europe, visiting and studying collections of Egyptian antiquities, and was appointed Conservator of the Egyptian Collections in the Louvre in 1826 (they were opened on 15 December 1827). In 1828–29 he visited Egypt to begin the first systematic survey of the monuments. On his staff were a number of people destined to

Pioneers of decipherment. *Left, above*, Baron Antoine Isaac Silvestre de Sacy, on a medal marking his death in 1838, by Depaulis; *left, below*, Thomas Young, after a portrait by Sir Thomas Lawrence; *below*, Jean François Champollion, painted by Léon Cogniet in 1831

become well known as early Egyptologists, notably the Italian Ippolito Rosellini (1800–1843), whose vast work, *I Monumenti dell'Egitto e della Nubia*, was published in 1832–44, and Nestor L'Hôte (1804–42), who contributed drawings to both Champollion's and Rosellini's works (see p. 130).

A number of British travellers, all variously associated with one another, visited Egypt in the mid 1820s. Frederick Catherwood (1799–1855), who is better known for his drawings of Maya monuments, went to Egypt for the first time in 1823–24 with Henry Westcar [73, 76]. In Malta on the return journey he met Robert Hay (1799–1863), a Scottish antiquary, who was fired with enthusiasm by his drawings and set off for Alexandria, where he landed in November. Hay made several journeys to Egypt, accompanied by a number of artists; Catherwood was in his party in 1832. The collections of drawings of sites, monuments and objects that Hay made (for he was a good draughtsman himself), and commissioned, form an invaluable archive which includes much material since destroyed or substantially changed.

With Hay on his first visit in 1824, and subsequently, was Joseph Bonomi (1796–1878), who was also a friend of Catherwood. A draughtsman and sculptor born in Rome of a family of architects, he was to stay for eight years, and many contemporary scholars called upon his fine and accurate drawing [79]. Bonomi prepared the illustrations for Wilkinson's *Manners and Customs of the Ancient Egyptians* (1837), joined the German expedition led by Richard Lepsius in 1842–45, set up the Egyptian Court at the Crystal Palace, London, in 1853, drew the sarcophagus of Seti I in Sir John Soane's Museum for publication in 1864, and cut the first hieroglyphic fount in England, for Samuel Birch's *Egyptian Dictionary* (1867). In 1861 he was appointed Curator of the Soane Museum, a post he held until his death. He was a man of prodigious energy, being always involved in numerous projects at the same time.

Another draughtsman who worked for Hay and Wilkinson was Edward William Lane (1801–76), who went to Egypt in 1825 for health reasons. Lane was particularly adept with the *camera lucida*, using it to record monuments [10, 75] and fine details of inscriptions. A skilled Arabist, he published *Manners and Customs of the Modern Egyptians* in 1836, and in 1838–40 his well known translation of the *Thousand and One Nights*.

A. C. T. E. Prisse d'Avennes (1807–79), who held an engineering appointment from Mohammed Ali in Egypt from 1826 to 1836, was an artist with engineering qualifications. He had a house and garden in Luxor, and his own boat on the Nile, from which he flew the Union Jack – claiming that his ancestry was Welsh, and his real name 'Price of Avon'. Extremely prolific in his output of pictures [38, XXIII], he published a two-volume *Histoire de l'Art Egyptien, d'après les monuments*, in 1858–77. Among his major discoveries was the Table of Kings, found at Karnak in 1845 and taken to France.

The flow of visitors continued in the 1830s. George Alexander Hoskins (1802–63) made numerous drawings in 1832–33 [55] – and again on a much later tour in 1860–61. Owen Jones (1809–74) visited Egypt in 1833 with Jules Goury, as part of a tour from Greece through Constantinople and the Levant, ending in Spain. His *Scenery of the Nile* (1840) and *Views on the Nile* (1843) are interesting less for drawings of entire buildings than for architectural details and topographical views [21, 48, 67]. Jones was particularly interested in polychromy: he designed the colour scheme for the Crystal Palace at the Great

Exhibition of 1851, and worked with Bonomi and Samuel Sharpe (an early Egyptologist) on the *Handbook to the Egyptian Court* (1854), which Bonomi had designed for the re-erected Crystal Palace at Sydenham. A few years after Jones, in 1837–38, Colonel Howard Vyse worked at Giza. His artist, Edward J. Andrews, produced plans and sections of the pyramids, as well as some interior views [13], and also drawings of Campbell's Tomb at Giza, for Vyse and Perring's *Operations carried on at the Pyramids of Gizeh* (1840–42).

David Roberts (1796–1864) was the first artist deliberately to set out for Egypt – and the Holy Land – with the express intention of making sketches and drawings to be worked up later into pictures for sale. Born in Edinburgh and trained initially as a house painter and theatrical scene painter, he moved to London in 1822 and painted his earliest historical picture, *The Departure of the Israelites,* in 1829 (p. 177). In 1823–33 he travelled in Spain, and in August 1838 he set out for Alexandria. He stayed in Egypt until February 1839, then left with two companions for Petra and Jerusalem. The journal which Roberts kept during his tour is full of comment on the people and the monuments as his hired boat made its way up the Nile to the Second Cataract. His drawings and oils of the monuments are delightful and accurate records, as he now realized an ambition he had held for a number of years. Often the monuments only serve as a background for carefully observed studies of the colourful natives [VII]. Roberts' interests extended beyond ancient Egypt and he spent a fortnight in Cairo making drawings and sketches of the mosques and street scenes. In order to do this without undue hindrance he adopted Turkish dress (as most early travellers did), shaved off his whiskers and forebore to use brushes of hogs' hair so as not to offend the religious susceptibilities of the Muslims. Certain sites so took his eye that he made several sketches from different angles and at different times of the day; he was particularly attracted by Dendera [X], Karnak [XI], Edfu [XXI] and Philae [XXIV, XXVI], and by views taken from under porticos [XXV]. After his return from the Near East his material formed the basis of a splendid series of lithographs by Louis Haghe. The Egyptian ones were first published in 1846–50 in large format, variously coloured, and then appeared in a reduced size in monochrome in 1855–56, with slightly different texts by William Brockedon.

Roberts was extremely prolific: several hundred of his sketches, plus many of his watercolours and oil paintings, have survived. A number of them are unsigned, but they are generally quite distinctive. He was elected a Royal Academician in 1841. After his death, the Art-Union of London commemorated him with a bronze medal issued in 1875 which translated his famous picture *The Letter Writer* into metal. It is a charming scene of a partly veiled woman dictating a letter to an elderly scribe in the *souk* in Cairo.

After the *Description de l'Egypte*, the other great scholarly work of the 19th century came from Germany: the *Denkmäler aus Aegypten und Aethiopien*, edited by Richard Lepsius, published in Berlin in twelve folio volumes in 1849–59. Lepsius (1810–84) is generally recognized as the only Egyptologist who can be ranked with Champollion. A brilliant linguist and methodical scholar, he led the Prussian expedition to Egypt and Nubia in 1842–45, on which the *Denkmäler* was based, and on a later visit in 1866 discovered the Edict of Canopus at Tanis, a bilingual stone which confirmed the basic correctness of Champollion's system.

Bronze medal commemorating David Roberts, by G. Morgan, issued by the Art-Union of London in 1875

The *Denkmäler* is more detailed than the *Description* in its recording of inscriptions and monuments [7, 18, 25, XVI], although the latter is on the whole much stronger in its representation of the sites. The Prussian expedition not only recorded but also excavated, notably at the site of the Labyrinth at Hawara [20], and also collected objects. Over 15,000 antiquities and casts were sent back to Berlin, where Lepsius later directed the building of the Egyptian Museum. Many of the items were featured in the *Denkmäler*'s 894 folio plates. Most of the drawings from which the plates were made were the work of Ernst Weidenbach (1818–82), who was the major artist with Lepsius's expedition. After returning from Egypt Weidenbach joined the staff of the Berlin Museum, where he worked until ill-health forced his resignation in 1878. His drawings were also used to illustrate other books by Lepsius and some of the publications of Georg Ebers and Auguste Mariette. As to the text of the *Denkmäler*, it was not published until after Lepsius's death, and then only from his notes, by the Swiss Egyptologist Edouard Naville (in five volumes, 1897–1913).

The members of the Prussian expedition occasionally broke away from their meticulous recording of the monuments to record very human emotions. Lepsius wrote home:

Karl Richard Lepsius, from a daguerrotype of 1850

Yesterday, the 15th of October, was His Majesty's birthday. I had determined on this day for our first visit to the great pyramid. There we would hold a festival in remembrance of our king and country with a few friends. We invited the Austrian Consul Champion, the Prussian Consul Bokty, our learned countryman Dr. Pruner, and MM. Lieder, Isenberg, Mühleisen, and Krapf to this party, at which, however, it is to be regretted that some were not able to assist. . . . a spacious gaily-decked tent came down, which I had hired in Cairo. I had it pitched on the north side of the pyramid, and had the great Prussian standard, the black eagle with a golden sceptre and crown, and a blue sword, on a white ground, which had been prepared by our artists within these last few days, planted before the door of the tent.

About thirty Bedouins had assembled around us in the interval, and awaited the moment when we should commence the ascent of the pyramid, in order to assist us with their powerful brown arms to climb the steps, about three or four feet in height [see p. 55]. Scarcely had the signal for departure been given, ere each of us was surrounded by several Bedouins, who tore us up the rough steep path to the apex like a whirlwind. A few minutes afterward our flag floated from the top of the oldest and highest of all the works of man with which we are acquainted, and we saluted the Prussian eagle with three cheers for our king. Flying toward the south, the eagle turned its crowned head homeward to the north, whence a fresh breeze was blowing, and diverting the effects of the hot rays of the noontide sun. We too, looked homeward, and each remembered aloud, or quietly within his own heart, those whom he had left behind, loving and beloved.

William Henry Bartlett (1809–54), who specialized as a topographical artist, travelled widely in Europe and America, and went to Egypt in 1845 [XVII]. His account, *The Nile Boat* (1850), was very popular, running to several editions. His work is noted for its realism and also because much that he drew has since been destroyed or considerably damaged. He himself perished in the Mediterranean on a voyage from Malta to Marseilles.

In November 1849 Gustave Flaubert (1821–80) arrived in Alexandria with his friend Maxime Du Camp (1822–94). Flaubert, not yet a novelist, was officially

on a mission from the French Ministry of Commerce, and Du Camp was commissioned by the Institut de France to record the monuments, using traditional techniques such as tracing and making 'squeezes' (paper moulds of incised inscriptions), but also taking what the Institut called 'this modern travelling companion, efficient, rapid, and always scrupulously exact' – a camera. The two men spent the winter in Cairo, and in true Romantic spirit camped overnight at Giza to see the sunrise from the top of the Great Pyramid.

On 6 February 1850 Flaubert and Du Camp set off in their hired *kanja*, the plan being the usual one – to sail up the Nile with the wind, then drift back with the current, stopping off at leisure. In Cairo, Flaubert learned, European clothes (consisting largely of layers of warm flannel) commanded more respect, but on their travels they wore Egyptian costume. Their boat, of the general type used by Nile travellers into the age of the steamer [38], was painted blue;

its *raïs* [captain] is called Ibrahim. There is a crew of nine. For quarters we have a room with two little divans facing each other, a large room with two beds, on one

Georg Frey, *The Prussian Expedition celebrating the birthday of King Friedrich Wilhelm IV on top of the pyramid of Cheops, 15 October 1842.* Lepsius is on the left, wearing a light-coloured smock

51

side of which there is a kind of alcove for our baggage and on the other an English-type head; and finally a third room where Sassetti [Du Camp's servant] will sleep and which will serve as a store-room as well. The dragoman will sleep on deck. The latter is a gentleman who hasn't doffed his clothes a single time since we have had him; he is always dressed in toile and always saying 'Il fa trop chaud.'

Seven weeks later they reached the farthest point of their journey, Wadi Halfa at the Second Cataract. The return took three months. They paused at nearly every site that bordered the great river, and made an exhausting side trip to Koseir on the Red Sea, during which they experienced the *simoon* or *khamsin* (p. 32). They reached Cairo in late June, and in July left Egypt for Beirut.

Photography was eventually, of course, to replace drawing as the normal record of a tour, but in its early days it was still too complicated. Du Camp suffered for his calotypes, and Francis Frith, who visited Egypt for the first time in 1856, had for his collodion process to carry glass plates and a virtual chemist's shop. Frith's photographs were popular, but there was still room for the artist.

Edward James Hawker travelled in Egypt in 1850–52 in search of health, and made many drawings of the monuments, of which three volumes are in the Griffith Institute at Oxford [51, 70, 72]. At about the same time Edward Lear (1812–88) – who is far more widely known for his nonsense verses for children – made his first visit to Egypt. He was there repeatedly between spells in Greece, in 1850–55 [6, 62], 1856–60, and after 1864 [15, 78]. Lear's Greek portfolio is vast, but his Egyptian subjects are rarer and have never been fully documented, and while he published books on his travels in Greece he left his Egyptian journeys unrecorded. Many other artists visited Egypt in the later 19th century, producing attractive work which is virtually unknown; they include Canon George Frederick Weston (1819–87), whose delightful watercolours are in the Fitzwilliam Museum, Cambridge.

Among 19th-century travellers who wrote of their experiences one stands out especially vividly – Amelia Ann Blanford Edwards (1831–92), the English authoress of many articles and novels in her journalistic career. As a child she had been fired with an enthusiasm for ancient Egypt by Wilkinson's *Manners and Customs*. This culminated in a visit to Egypt and Syria in 1873–74, the account of which was first published in 1877 and is her best-known book, *A Thousand Miles up the Nile*. It ran to several editions and is delightful and fascinating reading, second only perhaps to Belzoni's *Narrative*.

Amelia Edwards' experience as a journalist stood her in good stead and she lectured widely on Egypt, stirring up interest with her enthusiasm. A lecture tour in America in 1889–90 was highly successful, and the lectures were published in 1891 as *Pharaohs, Fellahs and Explorers*, which also appeared in several editions. She was much concerned with the need for scientific exploration and recording of the monuments before they were lost forever: many had disappeared in the seventy years between Denon's visit and hers. In March 1882 she was instrumental in founding the Egypt Exploration Fund – later Society – with Reginald Stuart Poole and Sir Erasmus Wilson (who had paid for Cleopatra's Needle to be brought to London in 1877). She was the Fund's first Secretary and publicist. On that foundation the Society flourished and is still a major influence in Egyptological excavation and studies today. Never a wealthy woman, she determined in 1885 to establish the first Chair of

Amelia B. Edwards, from the photograph used as frontispiece to her *Pharaohs, Fellahs and Explorers*, 1891

Egyptology in England, at University College London, and endowed it in her will. She hoped that Flinders Petrie (1853–1942) would be the first holder of the Chair, which he was for forty years until his retirement in 1933.

As the 19th century wore on, Egypt had become more accessible to anyone with enough interest who decided to make the journey. Many members of the royal families of Europe were present for the opening of the Suez Canal in November 1869. The Prince and Princess of Wales (later King Edward VII and Queen Alexandra) took a keen interest in antiquities. In 1862 he had observed the discovery of a mummy at Thebes (no doubt thoughtfully laid on specially), and in 1903 he presented the great funerary papyrus of Pinedjem II to the British Museum. The Emperor of Austria, Franz Joseph, was rather more energetic, as the sketch by William Simpson (a famous artist-reporter) shows. *The Illustrated London News*, which published the sketch on Christmas Day 1869, noted that when the Emperor visited Egypt he was 'no more of a great personage at the Pyramid than any of the crowd who now so often visit that wonderful structure'. In fact, in the hands of two strong Arabs who assisted his ascent, 'as he was pushed and pulled up over its huge stones he looked like a captive in the hands of his enemies; and he seemed for the moment to be very ill-used'. Immediately in the wake of the Prince and Princess of Wales Thomas Cook took his first party on the Nile, and had soon set up regular tours. Simpson's journalistic pencil captured other visitors hastening past the monuments [4]. Egypt had become the place to visit.

*Left* William Simpson, *The Emperor of Austria ascending the Great Pyramid*, 24 November 1869

*Below* A bronze medallion commemorating the Emperor Franz Joseph's presence at the opening of the Suez Canal: an Egyptian queen seated on a sphinx is flanked by the pyramids of Giza and a steam- and sail-powered ship

*Opposite, above* Discovery of a Mummy in an excavation near Thebes in the presence of H.R.H. The Prince of Wales, 18 March 1862, from Samuel Birch, *The Papyrus of Nas-khem*, 1863

*Opposite, below* William Simpson, *Dhahabîa of the Prince and Princess of Wales on the Nile*, at Philae, February 1869 (detail)

55

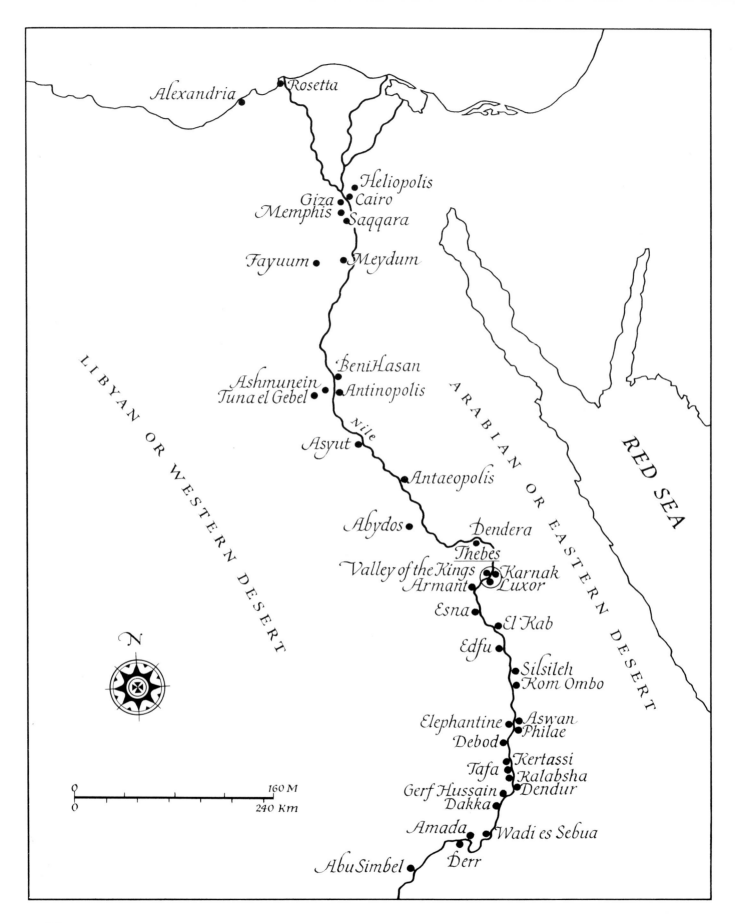

CONQUÊTE DE LA
BASSE EGYPTE
AN VII.

# Alexandria

*See also Pls. IV, VI*

'The two obelisks, of which the one still standing is named Cleopatra's Needle, are much disintegrated on the weather side, and in parts have become quite illegible. They were erected by Tuthmosis III in the sixteenth century BC; at a later period, Ramses Miamun [Ramesses II] has inscribed himself . . .'

Richard Lepsius, *Discoveries in Egypt*, 1853

1 Cécile, *Cleopatra's Needles and the Tower of the Romans from the south-west*, 1798, from the *Description de l'Egypte*

*Both obelisks had originally been set up at Heliopolis (see pp. 60–61) by Tuthmosis III in c. 1468 BC as monuments to his 'father', the sun-god Ra-Herakhti. The Roman emperor Augustus took them in c. 10 BC to Alexandria, where they were re-erected in front of the temple to the deified Julius Caesar, resting on the backs of inscribed bronze crabs, symbols of the Roman sun god Sol. It is curious how they both became known as 'Cleopatra's Needle', and have been so called since the Middle Ages. Cleopatra committed suicide in 30 BC, some twenty years before Augustus moved them to Alexandria.*

*During a great earthquake in AD 1301, one obelisk fell and, miraculously, remained intact. At the time of the British Army's successes in Alexandria in 1801 the Earl of Cavan cast covetous eyes on it as a fitting memorial of the campaign.*

Mohammed Ali generously presented it to Britain in 1820, but it was not removed until September 1877; finally, after various adventures at sea, it was erected in London in September 1878. Its companion that had remained standing was offered to America by the Khedive Ismail at the opening of the Suez Canal in 1869. It was removed to New York by the intrepid Lieutenant-Commander Henry H. Gorringe and erected in Central Park in January 1881. Since Lepsius's day both obelisks have suffered even further from weathering in their northern homes. Their fascinating history has been most recently told by Labib Habachi.

Very little remains of Alexander's great city except for the area around Pompey's Pillar (Pl. V), the recently excavated theatre and the catacombs. Much of it has disappeared into the sea over the centuries. The catacombs are unlike those of ancient Rome: in Alexandria they are quite ornate, many of them decorated with reliefs showing the ancient Egyptian gods – such as the jackal-headed Anubis, god of embalming – officiating, but now in Graeco–Roman guise. Ptolemy I provided a sumptuous tomb for Alexander the Great's body, which Augustus actually saw when he visited Alexandria. Since then the site has been lost, also probably under the sea, and nothing has ever been found that can be associated with his funerary equipment which, no doubt, was as magnificent as that in the recently discovered Macedonian royal tomb at Vergina in northern Greece.

2 Luigi Mayer, *Interior view of the catacombs at Alexandria*, from his *Views in Egypt*, 1804

# Heliopolis

'On the 13th of October we made a trip to the ruins of Heliopolis, the Biblical On, whence Joseph took his wife Asnath, the daughter of a priest. Nothing remains of this celebrated city, which prided itself on possessing the most learned priesthood next to Thebes, but the walls, which resemble great banks of earth, and an obelisk standing upright, and perhaps in its former position. This obelisk possesses the peculiar charm of being by far the most ancient of all known obelisks; for it was erected during the Old Empire by King Sesurtsen I, about 2300 BC . . . Boghos Bey has obtained the ground on which the obelisk stands as a present, and has made a garden round it. The flowers of the garden have attracted a quantity of bees, and these could find no more commodious lodging than in the deep and sharply cut hieroglyphics of the obelisk . . . three sides bear the same incription, and the fourth is only slightly varied.'

Richard Lepsius, *Discoveries in Egypt*, 1853

3 Luigi Mayer, *An Ancient Obelisk at Matarea, formerly Heliopolis,* c. 1800

4 *Opposite* William Simpson, *Heliopolis, – As it is,* 1878

*Heliopolis was the sacred city of the sun god, where a pyramidal stone known as the* benben, *the fetish of the god, was especially venerated. The shape of that stone was the origin of the obelisk – almost a pyramid up in the air. Many obelisks were erected at Heliopolis, of which this one, set up by Sesostris or Senusret I (1991–1928 BC) is the only survivor. One of only five obelisks still standing in Egypt, it is 20.4 metres (66 feet) high and cut from a single piece of red Aswan granite. Modern Heliopolis is now a fashionable suburb of Cairo; the obelisk rises at old el Matariya, almost forlorn in the fields with the native village nearby.*

# Giza

*See also Pls. I, VII, VIII*

'The officer who commanded the escort happened to be one of my friends; he entered me in the list of those who were bound for the pyramids; we were about three hundred . . . We sailed through the fields by the inundation trenches, and after tacking often through the cultivated country, we landed about noon on the borders of the desert, half a league from the pyramids. I took several views of them in different positions as we approached . . . In approaching these stupendous buildings, their sloping and angular forms disguise their real height, and lessen it to the eye . . . However, on attempting to measure any one of these gigantic works of art by some known scale, it resumes its immensity to the mind; for as I approached to the opening, a hundred persons who were standing under it appeared so small, that I could hardly take them for men.'

Vivant Denon, *Travels*, 1803

'Now stretching out before us is an immense plain, very green, with squares of black soil which are the fields most recently plowed, the last from which the flood withdrew: they stand out like India ink on the solid green. I think of the invocation to Isis: "Hail, hail, black soil of Egypt!" . . .

About half-past three we are almost on the edge of the desert, the three Pyramids looming up ahead of us. I can contain myself no longer, and dig in my spurs; . . . we climb rapidly up to the Sphinx, clouds of sand swirling about us.'

Gustave Flaubert, travel notes, 7 December 1849

6 Edward Lear, *The pyramids,* 1854

*Lear's painting shows, from right to left, the 4th Dynasty pyramids of Cheops (the Great Pyramid, built c. 2580 BC), of Chephren (c. 2560 BC), and of Mykerinus (c. 2540 BC). The Sphinx was carved for Chephren, and Barry's view shows it at the foot of the causeway that leads up to his pyramid.*

5 *Opposite* Charles Barry, *Pyramids of Geeza,* 1819

# Giza

## The pyramid of Cheops

*The Great Pyramid of Cheops or Khufu was rated as one of the Seven Wonders of the ancient world and is the only one still standing. Like its fellows it had been robbed in antiquity and had stood open at least since Classical times, when Strabo the geographer described it, explaining how the entrance had been closed by a pivoted stone in the outer casing. Most of that casing was subsequently removed in the Middle Ages for use in the buildings of what is now Old Cairo.*

*The Grand Gallery is a unique feature of this pyramid: the narrow corridor suddenly turns into a high, corbel-roofed passage that leads steeply up towards the burial chamber in the centre. Cécile's engraving shows it from the bottom looking up, and from the top looking back down.*

*Denon and Flaubert (and many others) were wrong in supposing that the sarcophagus had been hauled up here. Sir Flinders Petrie carried out a detailed survey of the Great Pyramid in 1880–82 and noted that the sarcophagus was an inch wider than the Ascending Corridor, hence it must have been placed in position before the burial chamber was roofed with its nine monolithic granite slabs. The south-east corner of the granite coffer has been broken away, presumably by early robbers; such is the workmanship in cutting the object from a single stone that it still makes a distinct bell-like sound when struck. No trace of a lid has ever been found, not even fragments on the floor of the burial chamber.*

'. . . you climb up a few feet, and directly find yourself at the bottom of a large and magnificent staircase, or rather inclined plane, one hundred and eighty feet in length, taking a direction upwards, and still towards the centre of the edifice: its breadth is six feet six inches . . . The sarcophagus must have ascended this passage, and the series of holes must have been intended to fix in some machine, to assist in raising such a heavy mass as the sarcophagus up so steep an ascent.

The side walls of this ascending gallery rise perpendicularly for twelve feet, and then form a sloping roof of an excessively high pitch . . . The whole height of this strange vault is therefore sixty feet from the part of the floor immediately beneath. [At the top of the gallery a low passage, once blocked by granite portcullises, leads to the burial chamber.] It must have required immense labour to construct this part of the edifice, and not less to have broken an opening through, so that the zeal of superstition has been opposed to the eagerness of avarice, and the latter has prevailed. After mining through thirteen feet of solid granite, a door, three feet three inches square, has been discovered, which is the entrance to the principal chamber . . . At the further end, to the right in entering this sanctuary, is a solitary sarcophagus, six feet eleven inches long, three feet wide, and three feet one inch and a half in height. When we have said that the tomb is a single piece of granite, and that the chamber is of the same material, half polished, and without cement, we shall have described all that is remarkable in this strange monument, which exhibits such rigid simplicity in the midst of the utmost magnificence of human power.'
Vivant Denon, *Travels*, 1803

7a,b Cécile *Two views of the Grand Gallery, Great Pyramid, Giza*, 1799, from the *Description de l'Egypte*

'After breakfast we visit the interior of the Pyramid. The opening is on the north. Smooth, even corridor (like a sewer), which you descend; then another corridor ascends; we slip on bat's dung. It seems that these corridors were made to allow the huge coffins to be drawn slowly into place. Before the king's chamber, wider corridors with great longitudinal grooves in the stone, as though a portcullis or something of the kind had been lowered there. King's chamber, all of granite in enormous blocks, empty sarcophagus at the far end. . . .

As we emerge on hands and knees from one of the corridors, we meet a party of Englishmen who are coming in; they are in the same position as we; exchange of civilities; each party proceeds on its way.'

Gustave Flaubert, travel notes, 8 December 1849

8 *Right* Luigi Mayer, *Chamber and Sarcophagus in The Great Pyramid at Gizah*, from his *Views in Egypt*, 1804 (detail)

# Giza

## The pyramid of Chephren

'In an intelligent age like the present, one of the greatest wonders of the world stood before us, without our knowing even whether it had any cavity in the interior, or if it were only one solid mass. The various attempts which have been made by numerous travellers to find an entrance into this pyramid, and particularly by the great body of French savans [*savants*], were examples so weighty, that it seemed little short of madness, to think of renewing the enterprise . . . With all these thoughts in mind I arose, and by a natural impulse took my walk toward the south side of the pyramid. I examined every part, and almost every stone. I continued to do so on the west – at last I came round to the north. Here the appearance of things became to my eye somewhat different from that at any of the other sides . . .

I observed on the north side of the pyramid three marks, which encouraged me to attempt searching there for the entrance into it . . . [After clearing much debris and finding a false entrance, Belzoni located the correct entrance framed by granite blocks.] My expectation and hope increased, as to all appearance, this must prove to be the object of my search. I was not mistaken, for on the next day, the 2d March [1818], at noon, we came at last to the right entrance into the pyramid . . . Having cleared the front of the three stones, the entrance proved to be a passage four feet high, three feet six inches wide, formed of large blocks of granite, which descended towards the centre for a hundred and four feet five inches at an angle of twenty-six degrees. [Difficulty was encountered in clearing the sloping passages and lifting some solid granite portcullises back into their sockets in the roof of the passages. Eventually Belzoni came to the end of the passages.]

I reached the door at the centre of a large chamber. I walked slowly two or three paces, and then stood still to contemplate the place were [sic] I was. Whatever it might be, I certainly considered myself in the centre of that pyramid, which from time immemorial had been the subject of obscure conjectures of many hundred travellers, both ancient and modern. My torch, formed of a few wax candles, gave but a faint light; I could, however, clearly distinguish the principal objects. I naturally turned my eyes to the west end of the chamber, looking for the sarcophagus, which I strongly expected to see in the same situation as that in the first pyramid; but I was disappointed when I saw nothing there. The chamber has a painted ceiling; and many of the stones had been removed from their places, evidently by some one in search of treasure. On my advancing towards the west end, I was agreeably surprised to find, that there was a sarcophagus buried on a level with the floor.

By this time the Chevalier Frediani had entered also; and we took a general survey of the chamber . . . It is cut out of the solid rock from the floor to the roof, which is composed of large blocks of calcareous stone, meeting in the centre, and forming a roof of the same slope as the pyramid itself. The sarcophagus is eight feet long . . . It is surrounded by large blocks of granite, apparently to prevent its removal, which could not be effected without great labour. The lid had been broken at the side, so that the sarcophagus was half open. It is of the finest granite; but, like the other in the first pyramid, there is not one hieroglyph on it.'

Giovanni Belzoni, *Narrative*, 1820

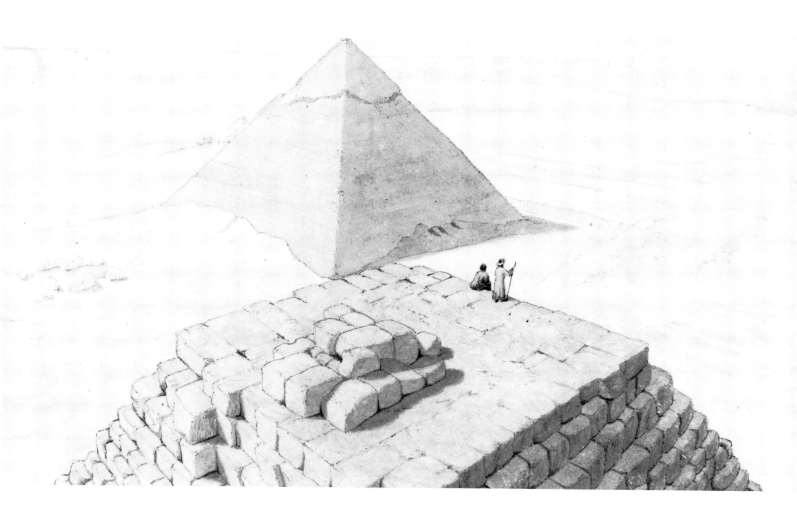

10 Edward Lane, *The Second Pyramid of Giza seen from above the top of the Great Pyramid at Giza* (drawn with the *camera lucida*), c. 1826–27

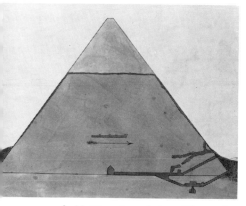

9, 11 *Opposite and above* Giovanni Belzoni, *Great Chamber in the Second Pyramid of Ghizeh* and *Section of the Pyramid*, 1818, from his *Narrative*, 1820

*Belzoni had a very good eye for any surface evidence of disturbance, as his career in Egypt repeatedly showed. In Edward Lane's drawing of the pyramid of Chephren, or Khafre, the three marks that Belzoni observed on the north – right – side, and the facing that survives at the top, are clearly visible.*

*In his section Belzoni shows an irregular robbers' tunnel attempting unsuccessfully to penetrate the mass. He entered by the upper passage (and carved his name on the slab above the opening). The lower passage was plotted by him from the inside, but the amount of debris outside prevented him finding the entrance in the pavement surrounding the pyramid. Nowadays tourists enter by the lower passage and leave by the upper, Belzoni's. The burial chamber which he is seen entering (and where he also inscribed his name) lies precisely below the centre of the pyramid. To commemorate Belzoni's success, friends and admirers in Britain commissioned a bronze medal.*

'Belzoni's chamber. At the far end, an empty sarcophagus. . . . Under Belzoni's name, and no less large, is that of a M. Just de Chasseloup-Laubat. One is irritated by the number of imbeciles' names written everywhere: on the top of the Great Pyramid there is a certain Buffard, 79 Rue Saint-Martin, wallpaper-manufacturer, in black letters . . .'
Gustave Flaubert, travel notes, 8 December 1849

# Giza
## The Sphinx

*See also Pl. I*

'I had only time to view the sphinx, which deserves to be drawn with a more scrupulous attention than has ever yet been bestowed upon it. Though its proportions are colossal, the outline is pure and graceful; the expression of the head is mild, gracious, and tranquil; the character is African; but the mouth, the lips of which are thick, has a softness and delicacy of execution truly admirable; it seems real life and flesh. Art must have been at a high pitch when this monument was executed; for, if the head wants what is called *style*, that is to say, the straight and bold lines which give expression to the figures under which the Greeks have disguised their deities, yet sufficient justice has been rendered to the fine simplicity and character of nature which is displayed in this figure.'

Vivant Denon, *Travels*, 1803

12 Vivant Denon, *Measuring the Great Sphinx at Giza*, 1798, from his *Voyage*, 1802

*The Great Sphinx forms part of the funerary complex of Chephren. Now once again completely cleared, it has always fought a losing battle against the encroaching sand of the desert. A stele between its paws records how the young prince Tuthmosis (later Tuthmosis IV, 1425–1417 BC) cleared away the sand in answer to a dream he had in the shadow of the Sphinx. In return the Sphinx promised him the crown of Egypt – obviously a subtle piece of propaganda to bolster the perhaps slim claim of a junior prince to the throne.*

'I carefully examined the third Pyramid whilst the people were at their dinners, and the result confirmed my opinion as to the position of the entrance . . . As soon as they [the workmen] were dismissed, Mr. Andrews and myself returned full of expectation to the mysterious entrance, impatient to examine what had excited the curiosity, and had hitherto been supposed to have eluded the researches of all explorers, and of which no tradition, ancient or modern, was known to exist.

[The blocking in the passage was rather more than Colonel Vyse had anticipated: it took two more days before they reached an antechamber at the end of which a further passage, formerly concealed, led them to the burial chamber.]

. . . The sarcophagus is supposed to have been originally placed in the centre of the chamber, to which its proportions were very similar, but it had been moved, and was found in the position represented. It was entirely empty, and composed of basalt, which bore a fine polish of a shaded brown colour, but was blue where it had been chipped off, or broken . . . It was finely carved in compartments . . . When the large apartment was finally cleared out, the greater part of the lid of the sarcophagus was found near the entrance of the passage descending to the sepulchral chamber; and close to it fragments of the top of a mummy-case (inscribed with hieroglyphs, and amongst them, with the cartouche of Menkahre) were discovered upon a block of stone, together with part of a skeleton . . . It would therefore seem that, as the sarcophagus could not be removed, the wooden case containing the body had been brought into the large apartment for examination.'

Colonel Howard Vyse, *Operations carried on at the Pyramids of Gizeh in 1837*, 1840–42, II

*The basalt sarcophagus of Mykerinus or Menkhare was the only decorated one from the three pyramids at Giza. It was carved with the 'palace façade' design, an architectural and artistic motif found in the Old Kingdom. The wooden coffin lid, of anthropoid shape, was in fact part of a later pious restoration of the burial, probably by the Saites in the 26th Dynasty (664–525 BC). It has been suggested that the sarcophagus may also have been a later restoration, copying an earlier style, which the Saites were very fond of doing.*

*Colonel Vyse decided, 'As the sarcophagus would have been destroyed, had it remained in the pyramid, I resolved to send it to the British Museum.' Fortunately it and the coffin lid were put on different ships. The ship carrying the sarcophagus foundered off Leghorn and has never been seen since. A few years ago an American attempt was made to locate and salvage the vessel, but without success, as it is in very deep water. The coffin lid arrived safely in London and was on show in the British Museum until recent years, when it was taken off display and put into store.*

# Giza
## The pyramid of Mykerinus

13 Edward J. Andrews, *Burial chamber of Mykerinus in the Third Pyramid at Giza*, 1837, from H. Vyse and J.S. Perring, *Operations carried on at the Pyramids of Gizeh*, 1840–42

# Giza
## Mastabas of the nobles

*The relatives of the king and other high court officials were buried in the* mastaba *tombs (Arabic for a bench, which they resemble) set out in 'streets' around the pyramids (compare Pl. VIII). It is from these tombs of the nobles of the 4th Dynasty that some of the finest statuary of the Old Kingdom comes, which is to be seen particularly in Cairo, Boston, and the Pelizaeus Museum at Hildesheim.*

'Of these [the tombs found by Lepsius at Giza] but few belong to the later time; nearly all of them were erected during or shortly after the building of the great pyramid, and therefore present us with an inestimable series of dates for the knowledge of the oldest definable civilisation of the races of man . . . The painting on the fine plaster is often more beautiful than could be expected, and occasionally exhibits the freshness of yesterday in perfect preservation. The subjects on the walls are usually representations of scenes from the life of departed persons, and seem mostly to place their riches, cattle, fish, boats, hunts and servants, before the eyes of the observer. Through them we became acquainted with every particular of their private life. The numerous inscriptions describe or name these scenes, or they set forth the often widely-extended family of the departed, and all his offices and titles, so that I could almost write a Court and State Directory of the time of King Cheops, or Chephren.'

Richard Lepsius, *Discoveries in Egypt*, 1853

14 Luigi Mayer, *Subterranean chamber, near the Pyramids at Geeza,* from his *Views in Egypt,* 1804

IX David Roberts, *Entrance to the caves of Beni Hasan*, from *Egypt and Nubia*, 1846–50

*The rock-cut chapels and tombs of the nomarchs – local 'war lords' – of the Oryx Nome, of the 11th and 12th Dynasties (2133–1786 BC), are particularly noted for their lively wall paintings and for their fluted columns, very proto-Doric in appearance (see also Ill. 21).*

X David Roberts, *Dendera Dec. 7th 1838*, from *Egypt and Nubia*, 1846–50

*For Dendera see pp. 97–101*

'It is not without something like a shock that one first sees the unsightly havoc wrought upon the Hathor-headed columns of the façade at Denderah. The massive folds of the head-gear are there; the ears, erect and pointed like those of a heifer, are there; but of the benignant face of the Goddess not a feature remains.'

Amelia B. Edwards, *A Thousand Miles up the Nile*, 1877

XI David Roberts, *Ruins of Karnack*, from *Egypt and Nubia*, 1846–50

*A view of the great temple complex of Amun looking north from the roof of the temple of Khonsu (Ill. 35). On the left is the huge Ptolemaic entrance pylon that faces the Nile; behind it in the first court is the column of Taharqa, followed by the Hypostyle Hall and the obelisks of Tuthmosis I and Hatshepsut; at the far right are a small Ptolemaic pylon and the sacred lake. The axis of the complex seen in this view is 500 metres (over a quarter of a mile) in length.*

XII David Roberts, *General View of the Ruins of Luxor from the Nile, 1838*, from *Egypt and Nubia*, 1846–50

*For Luxor see pp. 108–09*

'Luxor, the finest village in these environs, is also built on the site of the ruins of a temple, not so large as that of Karnac, but in a better state of preservation, the masses not having as yet fallen through time, and by the pressure of their own weight. The most colossal parts consist of fourteen columns of nearly eleven feet in diameter . . .'

Vivant Denon, *Travels*, 1803

'The long wall and house which join the two groups of columns is a granary . . . of the Pacha; and the structure which is seen behind the propyla is the minaret of a mosque. Under the columns, and in and about the Temple, are the huts and the houses of the Fellahs and other inhabitants . . .

Boats are seen on the river, that have brought to this scene of desolation travellers from a country which was probably uninhabited at the time when these temples had already passed through many ages of decay . . .'

William Brockedon, note to David Roberts, *Egypt and Nubia*, 1846–50

IX

X

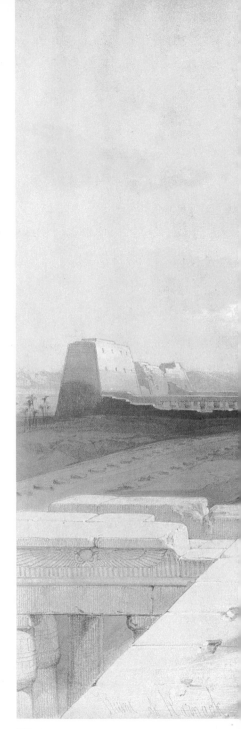

XI

XIII

XIV

XV

*A view taken from the top of the Horemheb colonnade. (It was only in March 1981 that the epigraphic expedition of the Oriental Institute of Chicago, who are recording that area of the temple, managed to put enough ladders together to emulate Roberts's little group on the left.) On the west bank can be seen, from left to right: Medinet Habu, the Colossi of Memnon, the Ramesseum and, far right, Gourna. From there the way winds through the hills into the Valley of the Kings, located behind the first line of hills and below the 'Lady of the Peak' in the centre (see Pl. XIX).*

XIII  David Roberts, *Lybian Chain of Mountains, from the Temple of Luxor*, from *Egypt and Nubia*, 1846–50

'How beautiful, how grand the approach to Luxor must have been, when these Obelisks stood before the colossal statues of Remeses II, one on either side of the approach to the stupendous pylons, enriched with sculpture and painting, by which the Temple was entered!'

William Brockedon, note to David Roberts, *Egypt and Nubia*, 1855–56 ed.

XIV  David Roberts, *Grand Entrance to the Temple of Luxor*, from *Egypt and Nubia*, 1846–50

'. . . the houses are on, in, or attached to the ruins. [They] are built among the capitals of columns: chickens and pigeons perch and nest in great lotus leaves; walls of bare brick or mud form the divisions between houses; dogs run barking along the walls. So stirs a mini-life amid the debris of a life that was far grander . . .

  The cornice of the pylons is badly damaged; only the part inside the door survives. On the two sides of the door, two colossi buried to the chest . . . The obelisk, in perfect state of preservation, is against the left-hand pylon. White birdshit streaks down from the very top . . . The obelisk that is now in Paris was against the right-hand pylon. Perched on its pedestal, how bored it must be in the Place de la Concorde!'

Gustave Flaubert, travel notes, 30 April 1850

*For a view with both obelisks in situ, see Ill. 39. The small domed building is the mosque of Abu Hagag.*

'This small but very beautiful Temple, which measures only sixty feet by thirty-three feet, is situated in a secluded valley, immediately behind the palace-temple of Medinet-Abou, and . . . has been used as a Christian church. The portico is supported by two lotus-headed columns, and at the extremities by two square columns attached to the wall: these are surmounted by the heads of Isis, or Athor.'

William Brockedon, note to David Roberts, *Egypt and Nubia*, 1855–56 ed.

XV  David Roberts, *Dayr el Medeeneh, Thebes*, from *Egypt and Nubia*, 1846–50

*The tiny Ptolemaic temple of Deir el Medineh lies just above the workmen's village of the same name. Essentially the workmen's temple, it was dedicated to Hathor as goddess of the dead and to Maat, goddess of truth and stability. Associated appropriately in the dedication were the great Egyptian architects who were deified long after their death: Imhotep of the 3rd Dynasty and Amenhotep son of Hapu of the 18th Dynasty. Both are represented on the reliefs in the temple, a very rare occurrence.*

# Memphis

'And now we are once more in the midst of the palm-woods . . . and the next moment we are all gathered round the brink of a muddy pool in the midst of which lies a shapeless block of blackened and corroded limestone. This, it seems, is the famous prostrate colossus of Rameses the Great . . . here it lies, face downward; drowned once a year by the Nile; visible only when the pools left by the inundation have evaporated, and all the muddy hollows are dried up. It is one of two which stood at the entrance to the great Temple of Ptah; and by those who have gone down into the hollow and seen it from below in the dry season, it is reported of as a noble and very beautiful specimen of the best period of Egyptian art.

Where, however, is the companion colossus? Where is the Temple itself? Where are the pylons, and the obelisks, and the avenues of sphinxes? Where, in short, is Memphis?'

Amelia B. Edwards, *A Thousand Miles up the Nile*, 1877

15 Edward Lear, *Colossus of Ramesses II at Memphis*, 15 March 1867

16 Dutertre, *French scholars measuring the fist of a statue of Ramesses II at Memphis*, 1798, from the *Description de l'Egypte*. This piece of sculpture is now in the British Museum.

*The area of Memphis, first capital of Egypt, still suffers from a high water-table, but the fine alabaster colossus of Ramesses II (1304–1237 BC) now reposes on its back in a specially designed pavilion. Discovered in 1820 by Caviglia and Sloane, it was given to Britain by Mohammed Ali and eventually raised by General Sir Frederick Stephenson. Wallis Budge, in* By Nile and Tigris, I, *tells how in the 1890s the statue was 'exchanged': public opinion, he was told, would not allow the colossus to leave Egypt, so a naos shrine dedicated to Horus of Philae, which Budge had found on the island, went to London instead. Lear sketched the statue in the dry season, placing a* fellah *at the tip of the head to suggest its overwhelming scale.*

# Saqqara
## The Step Pyramid

'As for the Pyramid in platforms (which is the largest at Sakkarah, and next largest to the Pyramid of Chephren) its position is so fine, its architectural style so exceptional, its age so immense, that one altogether loses sight of these questions of relative magnitude. If Egyptologists are right in ascribing the royal title hieroglyphed on the inner door of this pyramid to Ouenephes, the fourth king of the First Dynasty, then it is . . . the most ancient building in the world. It had been standing from five to seven hundred years when King Cheops began his Great Pyramid at Geezeh. It was over two thousand years old when Abraham was born. It is now about six thousand eight hundred years old according to Manetho and Mariette, or about four thousand eight hundred according to the computation of Bunsen. One's imagination recoils upon the brink of such a gulf of time.'

Amelia B. Edwards, *A Thousand Miles up the Nile*, 1877

17 J. Frey, *Step Pyramid, Sakkara*, 1842–44, from R. Lepsius, *Denkmäler*, 1849–59

*Curiously, Denon and Lepsius hardly noticed the Step Pyramid at Saqqara, although Lepsius was actually camped beside it for some time. It was built for Zoser, the second king of the 3rd Dynasty, c. 2670 BC, by his architect and vizier, Imhotep. The latter was to be deified in later ages, so revered were his memory and wisdom. Although Amelia Edwards was wrong in her dating and attribution – an illustration of how knowledge in the area has advanced in the last hundred years – she was correct in describing it as the oldest building in the world. A recent C-14 date for the megalithic tomb of Maes Howe in Orkney is a little earlier, but in its architectural sophistication Zoser's vast funerary complex must claim precedence. In the mid 19th century most of that ensemble around the pyramid was still buried under the sands.*

'The first journey brought me near the pyramid of Meidum, which I had already seen at a distance; I was now no more than half a league off it, but was separated from it by the canal of Jusef, and another smaller one, and we were not provided with a boat. However, with the assistance of an excellent glass, and as clear fine weather as possible, I was able to make my observations on it almost as well as if I touched it . . . In passing from the village of Meidum to that of Sapht, I had an opportunity of observing three sides of this pyramid, and it appears that an opening has been attempted at the second stage on the north side: the rubbish, covered with drifted sand, rises as high as this opening, and covers all but the angles of the first stage. The rise begins at the third stage, of which about a third part remains: the entire height of all that is left of this pyramid appears to be about two hundred feet.'
Vivant Denon, *Travels*, 1803

# Meydum

*The pyramid of Meydum, usually ascribed to Huni, last king of the 3rd Dynasty (c. 2613 BC), is the strangest and most enigmatic of all the Egyptian pyramids. It has been partly excavated by several expeditions, but there is still controversy as to how it acquired its curious shape; it seems to have collapsed some time before c. 1000 BC, and to have stood ever since in the rubble of its own limestone casing.*

*Although little excavation has yet been carried out in the cemeteries around it, they have yielded two of the best-known masterpieces of Egyptian art (now in the Cairo Museum): the 'pair statues' of Prince Rahotep and his wife Nofret, and the delightful painted Meydum geese.*

18 Ernst Weidenbach, *Meydum pyramid from the north-west*, 1842–44, from R. Lepsius, *Denkmäler*, 1849–59

85

# The Fayuum

'From the Labyrinth these lines come to you [25 June 1843] . . . There is a mighty-knot of chambers still in existence, and in the midst is the great square, where the Aulae stood, covered with the remains of great monolithic pillars of granite, and others of white, hard limestone, gleaming almost like marble . . .

Where the French expedition has fruitlessly sought for chambers, we found literally hundreds . . . supported by diminutive pillars, with thresholds and niches, with remains of pillars and single wall slabs, connected together by corridors, so that the descriptions of Herodotus and Strabo are quite confirmed in this respect; at the same time, the idea, never coincided in by myself, of *serpentine*, cave-like windings, instead of square rooms, is definitely contradicted . . .

. . . The fragments of the mighty pillars and architraves that we have dug out of the great square of the Aulae, give us the cartouches of the sixth king of the twelfth dynasty, Amenemha IV; thus is this important question answered in its historical position. We have also made excavations on the north side of the pyramid, because we may expect to discover the entrance there; that is, however, not yet done.'

Richard Lepsius, *Discoveries in Egypt*, 1853

The extensive buildings adjacent to the pyramid at Hawara that so excited the Classical commentators by their size and magnificent use of stone were part of the funerary complex of Amenemhet III (1842–1797 BC), the sixth king of the 12th Dynasty. His mortuary temple was the largest temple in the world, greater than those of Karnak and Luxor put together. Small wonder that it made such an impression in antiquity. Petrie eventually found the entrance of the pyramid and penetrated to the burial chamber during his excavations there in 1889–90.

20 *Above* Ernst Weidenbach, *Fayuum, view of the Labyrinth and pyramid*, 1842–44, from R. Lepsius, *Denkmäler*, 1849–59

Some of the monuments recorded by the French were drawn in the most adverse conditions: the savants, notably Denon, had to keep up with the cavalry. Sometimes an inspection of a temple had, of necessity, to be carried out at night by the light of flares, when they had bivouacked, as in the Fayuum temple seen here. Captain Head recommended that the best way of seeing the Theban temples was in such circumstances (p. 128) – and indeed Karnak by moonlight is a strange place, Gourna seen from the top of the pylons of Medinet Habu after sunset is a different world. The modern performance of Son et Lumière at Karnak brings the fantasy to life, but it still cannot surpass the silence of an Egyptian temple at night with just the dark sky and stars above it.

19 *Opposite* E. F. Jomard, *Egyptian temple at the eastern end of Lake Birket, Fayuum – an inspection at night by flambeau*, 1798, from the *Description de l'Egypte*

# Beni Hasan

*See also Pl. IX*

'It is remarkable how little Champollion seems to have attended to the monuments of the Old Empire. In his whole journey through Middle Egypt up to Dendera, he only found the rock graves of Benihassan worthy of remark, and those, too, he assigns to the sixteenth and seventeenth dynasty, therefore to the New Empire . . . It must then have been a proud period for Egypt – that is proved by these mighty tombs alone.'

Richard Lepsius, *Discoveries in Egypt*, 1853

*The rock-cut tombs of Beni Hasan excited much interest. Lepsius realized that they were of Middle Kingdom date, and also noted the confusion of other observers over the most famous painting there, the procession of Asiatics in the tomb of Khnumhotep: 'Champollion took them for Greeks when he was in Benihassan, but he was not then aware of the extreme antiquity of the monuments before him. Wilkinson considers them prisoners, but this is confuted by their appearance with arms and lyres, with wives, children, donkeys and luggage; I hold them to be an immigrating Hyksos family, which begs for a reception into a favoured land . . .' It was probably the fluted columns which occur in several of the tombs that misled Champollion into thinking they were of the Greek period.*

*The wall paintings are now badly damaged and it is not easy to pick out the procession of Semites, or the wrestling scenes that are a feature of the back walls of several of the tombs, including the one drawn by Owen Jones.*

21 Owen Jones, *Interior of a tomb at Beni Hasan*, 1832–33, from his *Views on the Nile*, 1843

# Antinopolis

'Stopped a short time at Sheik Abadé to examine the ruins of Antinoë – the site
of the town can with difficulty be traced by a great accumulation of soil to a
vast extent. It appears to have been divided into 4 parts by the two principal
streets at right angles and intersecting each other in the centre of the town
where there were probably 4 isolated columns – two of the columns are now
standing – they are Corinthian, the shaft plain except at the bottom where it is
encrusted with a series of long narrow acanthus leaves – they rest upon ill
proportioned pedestals, each having a Greek inscription now nearly illegible –
they are in very bad taste. The principal streets already mentioned have had
colonnades on each side and many of the shafts yet remain.'

Charles Barry, diary, 25 February 1819

'. . . all of it [is] sad, gray, desolate amid the dust. And yet only twenty years
ago there were three well-preserved Roman temples here, an entire portico, a
triumphal arch so lofty that the palm-trees rested their fruit-laden heads against
it, and the marble basins of sunken baths – in fact the monumental city
remained intact. But one day Ibrahim Pasha decided to build sugar refineries on
the opposite bank, near Roda; he laid his predatory hands on the Roman
buildings, tore them down, and used the stones for the construction of a
hideous factory.'

Maxime Du Camp, *Le Nil, Egypte et Nubie*, 1852

90

*Antinopolis, Antinoë or Sheik Abadé, was a rare (and much sketched) example of a complete Roman town in Egypt. It was built by the emperor Hadrian in AD 130 in memory of his young favourite, Antinous, who was drowned in the Nile near this spot. (It is said that he committed suicide by drowning to fulfil an oracle and save the emperor from disaster.) There is little left now beyond a scatter of columns and granite blocks.*

22 E. F. Jomard, *View of the ruins of Antinoë from the south-west,* 1798, from the *Description de l'Egypte*

23 *Right* Charles Barry, *Sheik Abadé,* 1819

Sheik abadé.

# Ashmunein

'In approaching the eminence on which is built the portico of Hermopolis, I saw its outline in the horizon, and its gigantic features. We crossed the canal of Abu-Assi, and soon after, passing across mountains and ruins, we reached this beautiful monument, a relic of the highest antiquity.

I was enchanted with delight at thus seeing the first fruit of my labours; for, excepting the pyramids, this was the first monument which gave me an idea of ancient Egyptian architecture; the first stones that I had seen which had preserved their original destination, without being altered or deformed by the works of modern times, and had remained untouched for four thousand years, to give me an idea of the immense range and high perfection to which the arts had arrived in this country . . . Is it the Egyptians who have invented and brought to perfection such beautiful art? This is a question that I am unable to answer; but even on a first glimpse of this edifice we may pronounce, that the Greeks have never devised nor executed anything in a grander style. The only idea which disturbed my enjoyment here was, that I must so soon quit this magnificent object, and that it required the hand of a master, and ample leisure, to do it justice with a pencil; whereas, my powers were humble, and my time measured out. But I could not quit it without attempting the sketch which I have given to my readers, which can but faint express the sensation which this noble fabric conveys, and which I sincerely hope some future artist will be enabled to finish under more fortunate circumstances.'

Vivant Denon, *Travels*, 1803

24 Vivant Denon, *The temple of Hermopolis*, 1798, from his *Voyage*, 1802

*Ashmunein, the ancient Khmunu, was a city sacred to the ibis-headed god of wisdom and writing, Thoth. Since the Greeks identified him with Hermes, the messenger of the gods, the later city incorporated the god's name as Hermopolis. Today the site is a series of mounds around the remains of a Christian basilica, much of the ancient town being under the modern houses nearby. The portico of the temple to Thoth that so caught Denon's eye was not, in fact, ancient Egyptian but built in the Ptolemaic period under Philip Arrhidaeus (323–317 BC), the half-brother of Alexander the Great. Only three column bases on the site now testify to its existence: in 1822 the grandeur that captivated Denon was burnt for lime, a fate that befell more than one Egyptian monument.*

'Perring, the pyramid measurer, has, in a recent publication, attempted to establish the strange notion, which I found also existed in Cairo, that the monuments of El Amarna were the work of the Hyksos; others wished to refer them to a period anterior to that of Menes, by reason of their certainly [*sic*], but not inexplicable, peculiarities; I had already explained them in Europe as contemporaneous kings of the 18th Dynasty.'
Richard Lepsius, *Discoveries in Egypt*, 1853

# Tuna el Gebel

25 Grach, *Rock-cut stele of Akhenaten at Tuna el Gebel*, 1842–44, from R. Lepsius, *Denkmäler*, 1849–59

*Lepsius, at least, took a rational and accurate view of the monuments of the 'heretic pharaoh' Akhenaten (1379–1362 BC) and located them in the correct dynasty. The American Egyptologist James H. Breasted once remarked that more ink has been spilt on the Amarna period than the whole of the rest of Egyptian history, and Akhenaten still continues to excite popular interest. The great stele cut into the rock face at Tuna el Gebel, west of the Nile, dated to Year 6 of his reign, is one of a series delineating the state boundaries of his new capital, Akhetaten. On the relief he appears with his queen, Nefert-iti, and two small daughters adoring the sun disk. On the left are fragmentary statues of the royal family.*

# Asyut

'Siut is a large well-peopled town, built, to all appearance, on the site of Lycopolis, or the city of the Wolf. – Why the wolf, which is an animal of northern climes, and is not found here! . . . No antiquities are found in this town, but the Lybian chain, at the foot of which it stands, here exhibits such a vast number of tombs, that without doubt this town occupies the territory of some very antient and flourishing city. We arrived here an hour after noon, and we employed the remainder of the day in procuring food for the army . . . I hastened to visit the Lybian chain of mountains, so eager was I to put my finger on an Egyptian mountain . . .

The rocks are excavated by a vast number of tombs of different dimensions, and decorated with more or less magnificence, and this too can leave no doubt of the proximity of the antient site of some considerable town. I took a drawing of one of the largest of these monuments . . . All the inner porches of these grottos are covered with hieroglyphs; months would be required to read them, even if one knew the language, and it would take years to copy them.'

Vivant Denon, *Travels*, 1803

Some particularly fine tombs of the Middle Kingdom have been found in the hills at the edge of the Western Desert, outside Asyut. Their inscriptions were still quite incomprehensible: when Denon went to Egypt in 1798 the future decipherer of hieroglyphs, Champollion, was only eight years old, and his discovery was not published until 1822.

26 Dutertre, *A French detachment marching into Asyut; in the background entrances to tombs cut into the mountainside*, 1798, from the *Description de l'Egypte*

27 Cécile, *Entrance to a large tomb outside Asyut*, 1798, from the *Description de l'Egypte*

# Antaeopolis

*The temple was built by Ptolemy IV and restored by the Roman emperors Marcus Aurelius and Lucius Verus. It was dedicated to Antaeus, the legendary wrestler whom Hercules overthrew and killed. The Greeks identified him with a local god, Anti, who is otherwise unknown. Twenty years after Dutertre drew the then substantial remains of the temple they had completely disappeared, being swept away by the Nile in 1821 when it changed its course. Excavations by the British School of Archaeology in 1923 recovered two fragments of an inscription recording the name of the god Anti, but otherwise little is still known about the area.*

28 Dutertre, *View of the temple of Antaeopolis – Quau el Kebir – from the west,* 1798, from the *Description de l'Egypte*

*Dendera, the ancient Tentyra, was dedicated to the cow-goddess Hathor, sister of Isis with whom she became conflated in late Egyptian mythology. The temple is, together with Edfu (Ills. 57, 58), the finest to survive in Egypt. Although the site had long been sacred, the present structure dates from Ptolemaic and Roman times. Begun in the reign of Ptolemy IX Soter II (116–107 BC), it was added to by most of his successors, including Cleopatra VII, of whom a famous relief appears on the outer rear wall. The Roman emperors Tiberius, Caligula, Claudius and Nero were all concerned with its decoration, and the names of Domitian, Nerva and finally Trajan (AD 98–117) appear carved in hieroglyphs on the entrance pylon.*

*All travellers were struck by the quiet repose of the Hathor-headed columns and the splendour of the relief decoration. Much had been severely defaced by the fanatical Copts who had built a large church within the temenos wall, between the entrance pylon and mamisi (birth-houses) and the temple façade.*

# Dendera

*See also Pl. X*

29 David Roberts, *Ancient Tartyrus (Dendera),* 1848

'Without, all was sunshine and splendour; within, all was silence and mystery.
A heavy, death-like smell, as of long-imprisoned gases, met us on the threshold.
By the half-light that strayed in through the portico, we could see vague
outlines of a forest of giant columns rising out of the gloom below and
vanishing into the gloom above. Beyond these again appeared shadowy vistas
of successive halls leading away into depths of impenetrable darkness. It
required no great courage to go down those stairs and explore those depths
with a party of fellow-travellers; but it would have been a gruesome place to
venture into alone.'

Amelia B. Edwards, *A Thousand Miles up the Nile*, 1877

30 J. Jollois and R. E. Devilliers
du Terrage, *Reconstruction of the
interior of the portico of the temple
at Dendera with a religious
procession taking place*, 1798, from
the *Description de l'Egypte*

98

31 Cécile, *Façade of the Great Temple at Dendera*, 1798, from the *Description de l'Egypte*

'In turning back to the right, I found buried in a gloomy heap of ruins a gate, built of enormous masses covered with hieroglyphs; and through this gate I had a view of the temple. I wish I could here transfuse into the soul of my readers the sensation which I experienced. I was too much lost in astonisment to be capable of cool judgement; all that I had seen hitherto served here but to fix my admiration. This monument seemed to me to have the primitive character of a temple in the highest perfection. Covered with ruins as it was, the sensation of silent respect which it excited in my mind appeared to me a proof of its impressive aspect, and without being partial in favour of the antique, I may add, that the whole army experienced similar feelings . . . I wished to take every thing on paper, but I could hardly venture to begin the work . . . I could not expect to find any thing in Egypt more compleat, more perfect, than Tentyra; I was confused by the multiplicity of objects, astonished by their novelty, and tormented by the fear of never seeing them again . . .

. . . I had just discovered, in a small apartment, a celestial planisphere, when the last rays of day-light made me perceive that I was alone here, along with my kind and obliging friend General Beliard, who, having satisfied his own curiosity, would not leave me unprotected in so deserted a spot.

[Denon visited the temple again when returning from Luxor.] As my time here was very limited, I began with what had been the principal object in my journey hither, the celestial planisphere, which occupies most of the ceiling of a little apartment, built over the nave of the great temple. The floor being low, and the room dark, I was able to work at it only a few hours in the day; but neither this, nor the multiplicity of the details, and the great care required in not confounding them by the necessity of viewing them in so inconvenient a posture, abated my ardour: the desire of bringing to the philosophers of my native country the copy of an Egyptian bas-relief of so much importance, made me patiently endure the tormenting position required in its delineation.'

Vivant Denon, *Travels*, 1803

100

It was the zodiac on the ceiling that excited most attention. The French determined to remove it – no easy task considering that it was part of a roof, some 2.5 metres wide and 1 metre thick (8 by 3 feet) and weighed in the region of 60 tons. It was removed in 1821 in the space of twenty-two days by the French master mason Lelorrain working with a small gang of Arabs, using small charges of gunpowder to make holes through the thick stone so that saws could then be used. The whole operation was a clandestine one, and Henry Salt was enraged since he had designs on it himself for William Bankes. The zodiac is now to be seen displayed in the Louvre, Paris, on the stairs leading to the lower Egyptian galleries. A plaster cast is in its place in the temple ceiling.

32 J. Jollois and R. E. Devilliers du Terrage, *Zodiac sculptured on the underside of the ceiling of a small room on the roof of the Great Temple at Dendera*, 1798, from the *Description de l'Egypte*. On the right is the figure of the sky goddess, Nut.

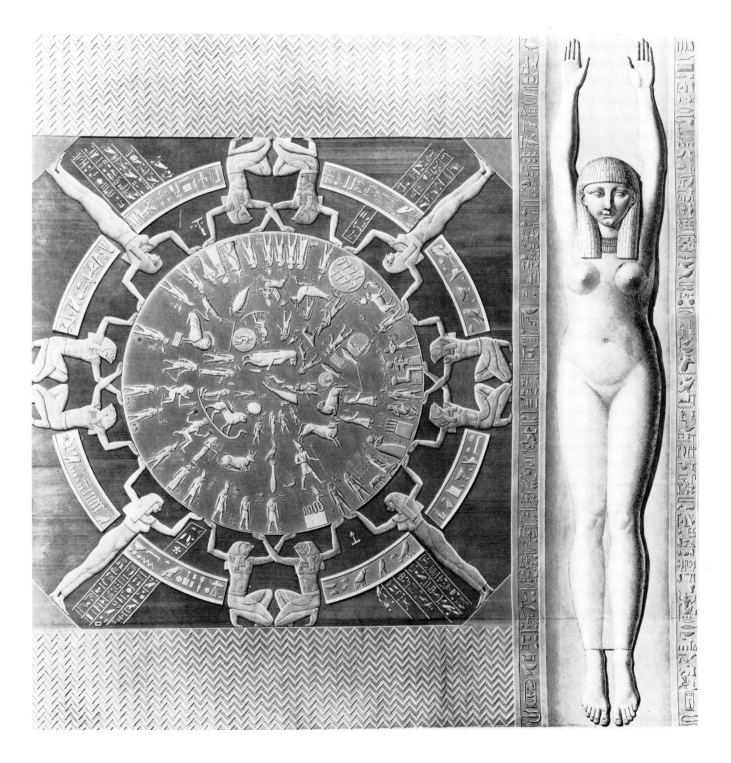

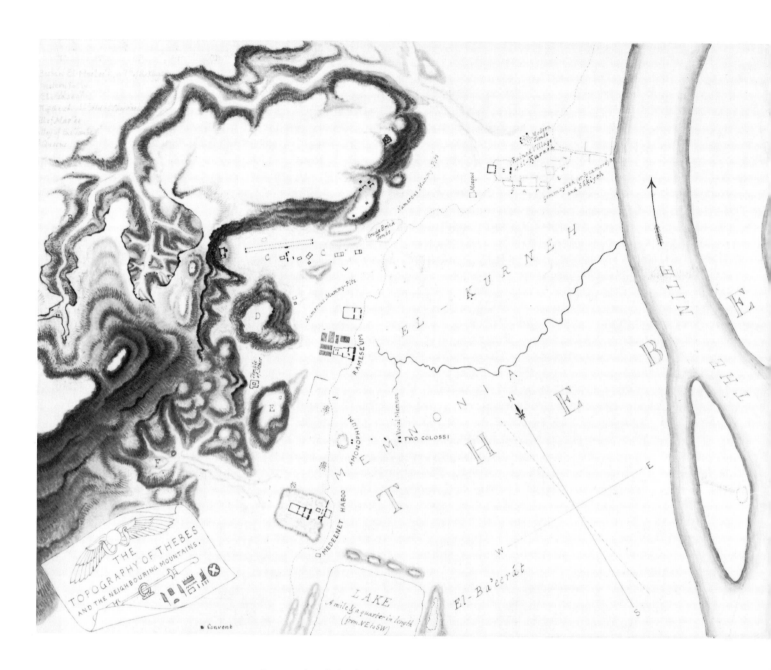

THE
TOPOGRAPHY OF THEBES,
AND THE NEIGHBOURING MOUNTAINS.

On the east bank (right) lie the temples of Karnak and Luxor, linked by a
processional way (Ill. 35). On the west, the ruins extend from Medinet Habu in the
south past the Colossi of Memnon and the Ramesseum to Gourna ('el-Kurneh') in
the north. The hills on the western edge contain the Valley of the Kings, reached by
a track from Gourna (compare Ill. 46).

# Thebes

'At nine o'clock, in making a sharp turn round the point of a projecting chain of mountains, we discovered all at once the site of the ancient Thebes in its whole extent; this celebrated city, the size of which Homer has characterised by the single expression of *with a hundred gates* [*Iliad IX*], a boasting and poetical phrase, that has been repeated with so much confidence for many centuries; this illustrious city, described in a few pages dictated to Herodotus by Egyptian priests, that have been since copied by every historian . . . the whole army, suddenly and with one accord, stood in amazement at the sight of its scattered ruins, and clapped their hands with delight, as if the end and object of their glorious toils, and the complete conquest of Egypt, were accomplished and secured by taking possession of the splendid remain of this ancient metropolis.

The situation of this town is as fine as can well be imagined; and the immense extent of its ruins convinces the spectator that fame has not magnified its size . . .'

Vivant Denon, *Travels*, 1803

*Ancient Thebes extended over a vast area on both sides of the Nile, encompassing Karnak and Luxor on the east bank, and the great mortuary temples (including the Ramesseum) on the west. It rose to real political and religious power when the princes of the area imposed their will on Egypt and founded the 18th Dynasty – marking the beginning of the New Kingdom – in c. 1567 BC. Their god Amun rose with them and was conflated with the sun god Ra to become Amun-Ra. At their high point the priesthood of Amun-Ra owned two-thirds of all temple land, 90 per cent of all ships, and 80 per cent of all factories.*

*In 663 BC the Assyrian Ashurbanipal sacked the city, a feat so unbelievable in the ancient world that the prophet Nahum could taunt great Nineveh, which fell in 612 BC, with 'Art thou no better than No-Amun [Thebes] . . . Ethiopia and Egypt were her strength, and it was infinite . . . yet she was carried away.' Diodorus Siculus visited the site in 57 BC and noted that the glorious tradition still survived: 'The Thebans boast that they were the most ancient philosophers and astrologers of any people in the world . . . There was no city under the sun so adorned with so many stately monuments, colossi and obelisks cut out of one entire stone.' Thebes revolted against Rome and was again reduced to ruins, but Strabo remarked in 24 BC that 'vestiges of its magnitude still exist which extend 9 miles in length . . . the spot is at present occupied by villages'.*

33 Edward Lane, *The Topography of Thebes and the neighbouring Mountains, c. 1826–27*

*All travellers since antiquity, like Denon and the French army, have been astounded and captivated by the ruins. Belzoni wrote in 1817, 'I seemed to be alone in the midst of all that is most sacred in the world . . . and it caused me to forget entirely the trifles and follies of life.' Today, away from the bustle of the modern town of Luxor, the same sense of wonderment and magnificence still pervades the atmosphere around the monuments of 'hundred-gated Thebes'.*

103

# Thebes
## Karnak

*Karnak, with its several temples, sacred lake and tumbled ruins within a great mud-brick temenos wall, is one of the most confusing of all the Egyptian temple sites. Like any great European cathedral, it was added to over the centuries, from the Middle Kingdom in the 20th century BC down to the time of Alexander the Great, when a shrine was added by his half-brother, Philip Arrhidaeus. Much restoration and renovation work is still being carried out.*

*Barry's drawing shows the southern approach, from Luxor (see Ill. 33): an avenue of sphinxes leads to a small pylon of Ptolemy III on the line of the temenos wall and, beyond it, the temple of Khonsu. In the distance is a side view of the great temple of Amun (compare Pl. XI); its massive entrance pylon, facing west towards the Nile, appears to the left of the temple of Khonsu, and a further series of pylons extend southward on the right.*

*Cécile's view, from the opposite side of the temple of Amun, is oblique: the axis of the temple runs diagonally from the entrance pylon, far right (west), through the Hypostyle Hall (Ill. 37), past the obelisks of Tuthmosis I and Hatshepsut, to the colonnaded court in the left foreground. Behind that are the craggy remains of the southern pylons and the small Ptolemaic pylon seen in Barry's drawing.*

34 Cécile, *General view of the temple of Karnak from the north-east*, 1798, from the *Description de l'Egypte*

35 *Opposite* Charles Barry, *Karnac, Upper Egypt* (view from the south towards the Ptolemaic pylon with the temple of Khonsu behind), 1819

'At length we arrived at Karnak, a village built on a small part of the site of a single temple, the circumference of which would, as has been somewhere noticed, require half an hour to walk around. . . . On examining the *ensemble* of these ruins the imagination is wearied with the idea of describing them. Of the hundred columns of the portico alone of this temple, the smallest are seven feet and a half in diameter, and the largest twelve. The space occupied by its circumvallation contains lakes and mountains. In short, to be enabled to form a competent idea of so much magnificence, it is necessary that the reader should fancy what is before him to be a dream, as he who views the objects themselves rubs his eyes to whether he is awake.'

Vivant Denon, *Travels*, 1803

'The first impression of Karnak is that of a palace of giants. The stone grilles still existing in the windows give the scale of these formidable beings. As you walk about in this forest of tall columns you ask yourself whether men weren't served up whole on skewers, like larks. In the first courtyard, after the two great pylons as you come from the Nile, there is a fallen column all of whose segments are in order, despite the crash, exactly as would be a fallen pile of checkers. We return via the avenue of sphinxes: not one has its head – all decapitated.'

Gustave Flaubert, travel notes, May 1850

*The great fallen column of Taharqa that Flaubert mentions has been re-erected. The sphinxes that he noticed, one of which Chabrol sketched, are those lining the western avenue from the Nile to the entrance pylon.*

36 Chabrol, *Headless sphinx in the avenue of sphinxes before the pylons at Karnak with an artist of the Commission making use of the shade*, 1798, from the *Description de l'Egypte*

37 *Opposite* David Roberts, *Interior of the Hypostyle Hall, Karnak*, 29 November 1838

# Thebes

## Luxor

*See also Pls. XII–XIV*

38 A. C. T. E. Prisse d'Avennes, *A 'kanja' on the Nile off Thebes (Luxor) the Temple of Luxor in the background, 1838–39*

'The Entrance to the Village of Luxor: what a striking mixture of beggary and magnificence! What a gradation of ages in Egypt is offered by this single scene! What grandeur and simplicity in the simple inspection of this picture! . . . I often came to meditate on this spot, to enjoy the past and the present, to compare the successive generations of inhabitants by their respective works . . .

The two obelisks of rose-coloured granite were still seventy feet above the ground . . . Their preservation is perfect, the hieroglyphs with which they are covered are cut deep, and in relief at the bottom, and shew the bold hand of a master and a beautiful finish: what an admirable temper must the gravers be that could touch such hard materials! What time required for the labour! What machines to drag such enormous blocks out of the quarries, to transport them hither, and to set them upright!'

Vivant Denon, *Travels*, 1803

The temple was cocooned within the mud houses of the modern village, but the French managed to extract the eastern (river side) obelisk and transport it to Paris in 1836. Not until 1885 could Sir Gaston Maspero begin to clear away the houses; old Mustapha Aga, the local British Consular Agent, who had a house built into the Horemheb colonnade, held out until his death in 1887. Only one intrusive building remained, and still does today – the small mosque in the first court (see Pls. XII, XIV), dedicated to the Muslim saint Abu Hagag who is credited with having introduced the True Faith into Egypt. The temple of Luxor must have one of the longest histories of religious veneration on a single site in the world, extending from the reign of Amenophis III (1417–1379 BC), who began building it, to the present day.

Prisse d'Avennes' watercolour shows his own boat on the river, and behind it, from left to right, the obelisks and pylon of Ramesses II, the tall Horemheb colonnade, and the lower colonnade of Amenophis III.

39 Charles Barry, *Entrance to the temple of Luxor with two obelisks of Ramesses II*, 1819

40 Edward Lane, *The Horemheb colonnade, temple of Luxor*, c. 1826–27

# Thebes
## The Colossi of Memnon

'Our attention was arrested in the plain by two large statues in a sitting posture, between which, according to Herodotus, Strabo, and those who have copied the relation of these writers, was the famous statue of Osymandyas, the largest of all these colossal figures . . . The two statues still existing are in the proportion of from fifty to fifty-three feet in height; they are seated with their two hands on their knees; all that remains of them shows a severity of style, and a straightness of position. The bas-reliefs and small figures clustered round the seat of the southernmost of these statues, are not without elegance and delicacy of execution. On the leg of the statue the most to the north, the names of the illustrious and ancient travellers who came to hear the sound of the statue of Memnon are written in Greek. We may here see the great influence which celebrity exercises over the minds of men, since, when the ancient Egyptian government and the jealousy of the priests no longer forbade strangers to touch these monuments, the love of the marvellous retained its empire over the minds of those that came hither as visitors.'

Vivant Denon, *Travels*, 1803

*The Colossi of Memnon are seated statues of Amenophis III (1417–1379 BC), and stood before his mortuary temple. Nothing else of it now remains apart from a stele some 400 metres (a quarter of a mile) behind them. In antiquity the northernmost of the statues – on the right – made a moaning sound at dawn and dusk and was identified with the hero Memnon who fled from Troy and died in Egypt: it was thought that he saluted his mother Eos with the noise. Many travellers testified to hearing it and three emperors of Rome visited it, Augustus, Hadrian and Septimius Severus. After repairs carried out during the reign of the latter (AD 193–211) the sound was not heard again. It was caused by the change of temperature at sunrise and sunset, possibly enhanced by the priests concealing something like a reed which vibrated in a crevice within the statue. The cartouches of Amenophis III on the sides of the thrones were used by Champollion in conjunction with the Rosetta Stone in his decipherment of hieroglyphs.*

41 Charles Barry, *Plain of Thebes – West of the Nile*, 1819

42 Henry Salt, *Statue of Memnon* (the northern figure, or 'vocal Memnon'), *c.* 1819

XVI Ernst Weidenbach, *View of the temple of Seti I at Gourna*, from R. Lepsius, *Denkmäler*, 1849–59 (detail)

*The superb, but now sadly little visited, temple of Seti I (1318–1304 BC) is on the right with the Ramesseum in the distance.*

XVII William Henry Bartlett, *Memnonium*, 1845

'Of all Theban ruins, the Ramesseum is the most cheerful. Drenched in sunshine, the warm limestone [actually sandstone] of which it is built seems to have mellowed and turned golden with time. No walls enclose it. No towering pylons overshadow it. It stands high, and the air circulates freely among these simple and beautiful columns. There are not many Egyptian ruins in which one can talk and be merry; but in the Ramesseum one may thoroughly enjoy the passing hour.'
Amelia B. Edwards, *A Thousand Miles up the Nile*, 1877

*The Ramesseum was the mortuary temple of Ramesses II (see pp. 122–23).*

XVIII Giovanni Belzoni, *Mode in which the Younger Memnon's head (now in the British Museum) was removed by G. Belzoni*, 1822

'As I entered these ruins, my first thought was to examine the colossal bust I had to take away. I found it near the remains of its body and chair, with its face upwards, and apparently smiling on me, at the thought of being taken to England. I must say, that my expectations were exceeded by its beauty, but not by its size . . . The Fellahs of Gournou [Gourna], who were familiar with Caphany, as they named the colossus, were persuaded, that it could never be removed from the spot where it lay . . . The mode I adopted to place it on the car was very simple, for work of no other description could be executed by these people, as their utmost sagacity reaches only to pulling a rope, or sitting on the extremity of a lever as a counterpoise. By means of four levers I raised the bust, so as to leave a vacancy under it, to introduce the car; and, after it was slowly lodged on this, I had the car raised in the front, with the bust on it, so as to get one of the rollers underneath. I then had the same operation performed at the back, and the colossus was ready to be pulled up.'
Giovanni Belzoni, *Narrative*, 1820

*Belzoni removed the bust from the Ramesseum in 1816, succeeding where the French had failed. But the work was done in July and August, the hottest time of the year, and Belzoni's strength did not preserve him from the consequences: on 28 July he records,*

'In the evening I was very poorly: I went to rest, but my stomach refused any aliment . . . On the next day, the 29th, I found it impossible to stand on my legs, and postponed the work to the day following . . . On the 30th we continued the work, and the colossus advanced a hundred and fifty yards towards the Nile. I was a little better in the morning, but worse again in the evening . . .'

XVI

XVII

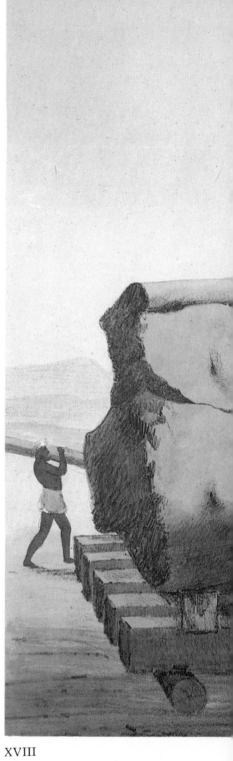

XVIII

XIX

XX

Kom Ombo
Nov 21st 1838

David Roberts R.A.

XXII

'Here the Pharaohs of Thebes were entombed . . . so ingeniously were some of them concealed, that it was only after a lapse of thirty-two centuries that the indefatigable Belzoni discovered some of them. His zeal and energy in Egyptian research were nowhere more remarkably displayed than in this retired valley . . . The most remarkable of these tombs, that which in the drawing is seen the second on the left, was discovered by Belzoni in 1817, and bears his name . . .'
William Brockedon, note to David Roberts, *Egypt and Nubia*, 1855–56 ed.

*'Belzoni's Tomb' was that of Seti I; above it rises the 'Lady of the Peak', visible from Luxor across the river (see Ill. 46, and Pl. XIII).*

XIX David Roberts, *Entrance to the Tombs of the Kings of Thebes, Bab el Malouk*, from *Egypt and Nubia*, 1846–50 (detail)

'In the centre of the town, near the market-place, is a magnificent Egyptian temple, the whole of which is however completely buried, and modern houses built over it, except the portico or anti-chamber; this is supported by twenty-four columns, in four rows of six each . . . The capitals, all of which are different, are well executed; they combine the representations of the fruit and leaves of the date, vine, lotus, &c.'
The Hon. Charles Leonard Irby and James Mangles, *Travels*, 1823

XX David Roberts, *Temple at Esneh, Nov. 25th 1838*, from *Egypt and Nubia*, 1846–50

*For Esna see pp. 136–37*

'Though half buried it is more beautiful than if laid open and reminds me of Piranesi Etchings of the Forum of Rome . . . I made two large drawings of the Portico [Ill. 57], and, from it, looking across the Dromos towards the Propyla. To do the first I was compelled to sit with my umbrella in the sun which today must have been 100 in the shade. I fear I did very wrong. I hope in God there may be no bad effects from it – but the Portico is so beautiful in itself I could not resist it. . . . for the future I shall avoid the sun even if I lose a subject.'
David Roberts, journal

XXI David Roberts, *The Outer Court of the Temple of Edfou, Egypt*, [1840]

*For Edfu see pp. 140–41*

'Perhaps no point in this vast edifice is made more striking by contrast, than the grand propylon, with a few mud huts which rest against it on the cornices of the colonnade that surrounds the court: they have scarcely more importance in the scene than swallows' nests under the gable of a modern dwelling.'
William Brockedon, note to David Roberts, *Egypt and Nubia*, 1846–50

'Kom Ombo is a magnificent torso. It was as large once as Denderah – perhaps larger; for, being on the same grand scale, it was a double Temple and dedicated to two Gods, Horus and Sevek; the Hawk and the Crocodile. Now there remain only a few giant columns buried to within eight or ten feet of their gorgeous capitals; a superb fragment of architrave; one broken wave of sculptured cornice, and some fallen blocks graven with the names of Ptolemies and Cleopatras.'
Amelia B. Edwards, *A Thousand Miles up the Nile*, 1877

XXII David Roberts, *Kom Ombo, Nov. 21st 1838*, from *Egypt and Nubia*, 1846–50

*For Kom Ombo see pp. 144–45*

# Thebes
## The Ramesseum
*See also pls. XVII, XVIII*

'At some paces from this gate [the entrance pylon] are the remains of an enormous colossus; it has been wantonly shattered, for the parts which are left have so well preserved their polish, and the fractures their edges, that it is evident, if the spirit of devastation in mankind had trusted to time alone to ruin this monument, we should still see it entire and uninjured. Suffice it to say, to give an idea of its dimensions, that the breadth of the shoulders is twenty-five feet, which would give about seventy-five for the entire height: the figure is exact in its proportions, the style middling, but the execution perfect; when overset, it fell upon its face, which hides this interesting part; the drapery being broken we can no longer judge by its attributes whether it is the figure of a king or a divinity. Is it the statue of Memnon, or that of Osymandyas? – the descriptions hitherto given of this monument throw more confusion than light upon this question. If it is the statue of Memnon, which appears to me the more probable, every traveller for two thousand years must have mistaken the object of their curiosity . . . One foot of this statue remains, which is broken off and in good preservation; it may be easily carried away, and may give those in Europe a scale of comparison of the monuments of this species . . . The spot where this figure stood might be either a temple or a palace, or both at the same time . . .

This ruin, which is situated on the slope of the mountain, and has never been inhabited in later times, is so well preserved in the parts that are still standing, that it appears more like a new and unfinished building . . . It would have taken some time and examination to have made out the plan of this temple, but the cavalry were galloping on, and I was obliged to follow them closely, not to be stopped for ever in my researches.'

Vivant Denon, *Travels*, 1803

*The Ramesseum, also known as the Memnonium from the identification of the colossal statue with Memnon (see pp. 110–11), was the mortuary temple of Ramesses II 'the Great'. Its huge statues and vast proportions had been mentioned by several travellers in antiquity. The name Osymandias, used in Classical times for Ramesses, appears to derive from his praenomen, User-maat-Re, which appears cut on the fallen statue. It has been calculated that the figure, carved from a single block, may originally have weighed about 1,000 tons. Denon ascribes its destruction to the hand of man and it is often said that it was overthrown by the Persians. The alternative explanation, that it fell in an earthquake in late antiquity, is supported by expert geological opinion based on the typical telltale 'twist' seen in the first pylon nearby.*

*Fortunately no one thought to take up Denon's idea of removing the colossal feet and they still stand in the first court of the temple with long grass growing over them and a shady tamarisk tree nearby. Shelley immortalized them and the statue in his sonnet 'Ozymandias':*

43 Charles Barry, *Memnonium, Upper Egypt*, 1819

> I met a traveller from an antique land
> Who said: 'Two vast and trunkless legs of stone
> Stand in the desert . . . Near them, on the sand,
> Half sunk, a shattered visage lies, whose frown,
> And wrinkled lip, and sneer of cold command,
> Tell that its sculptor well those passions read
> Which yet survive, stamped on these lifeless things,
> The hand that mocked them, and the heart that fed.
> And on the pedestal these words appear:
> "My name is Ozymandias, King of kings:
> Look on my works, ye Mighty, and despair!"
> Nothing beside remains. Round the decay
> Of that colossal wreck, boundless and bare,
> The lone and level sands stretch far away.'

*Little has changed on the site. Belzoni removed the other torso of Ramesses II, of red and black granite, to the British Museum in 1816 (Pl. XVIII), taking care – as instructed – not to try to remove the greater colossus; and it was a visit to the museum in the winter of 1817 to see this and other newly acquired Egyptian antiquities, combined with reading Diodorus Siculus, that inspired Shelley to write his sonnet.*

# Thebes

## Medinet Habu

44 Captain Charles Francklin Head, *Part of the interior of the temple of Medinah Habou,* January 1830

'At the north end of the court the central column has been cast down, and in its place there are the remains of a Christian church, the nave of which was supported by moderate sized pillars, a few of which are seen in the middle of the court, marking the art and the power of the two ages. "Poor and humble do they look in the midst of such ruins as these: but to the Christian eye they are arranged with glory." They are unpretending and shew the character of the early Christians, by whom they were designed . . . In the early days of Christianity there was a considerable church establishment and two bishoprics at Thebes, and there is every reason to conclude that this was the capital of the western diocese. Without the walls of this temple there are many pieces of fine sculpture, that vie with any in the other temples, though there is little unshrouded by rubbish, except the north wall, or that facing the Memnon, where the ornaments are of the most animated character.' [the great series of reliefs of the battles with the Sea Peoples]

Captain Charles Francklin Head, *Eastern and Egyptian Scenery, Ruins &c.,* 1833

124

'At the right, adjoining the village of Medinet-Abu, at the bottom of the mountain, is a vast palace, built and enlarged at different periods. All that I could make out of it in this my first examination on horseback, was, that the lower part of this palace which abuts against the mountain, is the most ancient in its construction, and is covered with hieroglyphics, cut very deep and without any relief; and that, in the fourth century, the catholic religion converted it to sacred purposes, and made a church of it, adding two rows of pillars in the style of the age, to support a covered roof. At the south of this monument there are Egyptian apartments, with ladders and square windows, the only building I had yet seen here which was not a temple; and beyond this are edifices rebuilt with old materials, but left unfinished.'

Vivant Denon, *Travels*, 1803

*The huge complex at Medinet Habu consists mainly of the mortuary temple of Ramesses III (1198–1166 BC), the largest that now survives on the west bank at Thebes. The portion covered with hieroglyphs 'without any relief' is the longest known hieroglyphic inscription, relating to the great battles with the Sea Peoples which occurred in Ramesses' reign.*

*Captain Head's watercolour shows the courtyard of the temple, where the early Christian columns contrast strangely with the massive Egyptian pillars. Barry's drawing is of the unique fortified entrance to the temple area, based on the design of Syrian forts (and thus known by their name,* migdol*), which Ramesses built to commemorate his conquests. Some of the apartments over the gateway appear to have been used for harem quarters as reliefs there show Ramesses dallying with various ladies.*

45 Charles Barry, *Supposed palace, Medinet Abou* (the *migdol*), 1819

# Thebes
## The Valley of the Kings

*See also Pl. XIX*

'The sacred valley, named Beban el Malook, begins at Gournou [Gourna], runs toward the south-west, and gradually turns due south. It contains the celebrated tombs of the kings of Egypt, and divides itself into two principal branches, one of which runs two miles farther to the westward, making five miles from the Nile to the extremity. The other, which contains most of the tombs, is separated from Gournou only by a high chain of rocks, which can be crossed from Thebes in less than an hour. The same rocks surround the sacred ground, which can be visited only by a single natural entrance, that is formed like a gateway, or by the craggy paths across the mountains . . . Some of these tombs are quite open, and others incumbered with rubbish at the entrance . . . Strabo may have counted eighteen, as may be done to this day, including some of an inferior class, which cannot be esteemed as tombs of the kings of Egypt from any other circumstance, than that of having been placed in this valley . . . Certain it is, that the tombs in the valley of Beban el Malook are in far better condition than those in Gournou.

Under these circumstances, reflecting on the possibility of discovering some of the tombs of the kings, I set the few men I had to work. On the 6th of October [1817] I began my excavation, and on the 9th discovered the first tomb.'

Giovanni Belzoni, *Narrative*, 1820

*Belzoni had an almost uncanny eye for the terrain and any disturbance of it, a gift he also displayed at the pyramid of Chephren. On his map the six tombs shown marked in solid black were discovered by him during his short period in the valleys. He did not, of course, know whose they were since hieroglyphs could not be read. Belzoni's finds were (his numbers, from top to bottom):*

WESTERN VALLEY

1 *Tomb of the pharaoh Ay (1352–1348 BC), successor of Tutankhamun. Modern no. 23.*
2 *Unnamed and uninscribed tomb. No. 24 or 25.*

EASTERN OR MAIN VALLEY

3 *Tomb of Ramesses I (1320–1318 BC). No. 16.*
4 *Unidentified tomb, possibly for relatives of Tuthmosis III or Queen Hatshepsut.*
5 *Tomb of Prince Mentuhirkhopshef, a son of Ramesses IX (1140–1123 BC). No. 19.*
6 *Tomb of Seti I (1318–1304 BC). No. 17.*

*The tomb of Seti I, the finest in the Valley, is decorated in vivid colours throughout its great length. Belzoni found the superbly carved alabaster sarcophagus of the pharaoh in the burial chamber, empty. It is now in Sir John Soane's Museum, London, and Seti's mummy, found in the great Deir el Bahari cache of royal mummies in 1881, in the Cairo Museum.*

*Belzoni tells how the governor of the district, Hamad Aga of Qena, hurried to the tomb – taking only 36 hours by land instead of the normal two days – drawn by stories of huge treasures being found. Disappointed to find them false, he sat*

*continued*

46 Giovanni Belzoni, *Topographical Map of the Valley of Biban Ell Malook, in which the Tombs of the Kings are situated, 1817, from his Narrative, 1820*

Plate 39

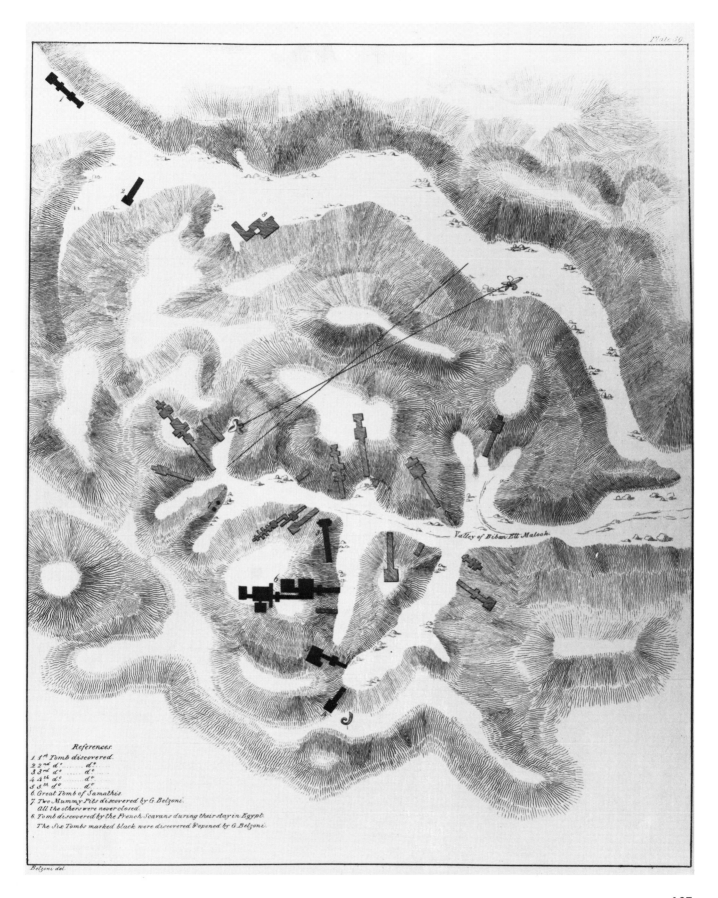

Valley of Biban Ell Malook.

References.
1 1st Tomb discovered.
2 2nd do. do.
3 3rd do. do.
4 4th do. do.
5 5th do. do.
6 Great Tomb of Samathis.
7 Two Mummy Pits discovered by G. Belzoni.
  All the others were never closed.
8 Tomb discovered by the French Savans during their stay in Egypt.
  The Six Tombs marked black were discovered & opened by G. Belzoni.

Belzoni del.

*himself down on the sarcophagus in the painted burial chamber. Belzoni continues, 'I asked him what he thought of the beautiful figures painted all round. He just gave a glance at them, quite unconcerned, and said, "This would be a good place for a harem, as the women would have something to look at."'*

*When Belzoni left Egypt in 1819 he considered that there were no more tombs to be found in the Valley. Subsequently, later last century Loret found major pharaohs' tombs, including Amenophis II and Tuthmosis III. Theodore Davis, the American Egyptologist, continued excavation early this century, finding amongst others the tombs of Horemheb, Hatshepsut and 'Queen Tiyi'. He left the Valley in 1912, similarly saying that it was exhausted. The last and greatest discovery came in 1922 with the finding of Tomb no. 62 – Tutankhamun – by Howard Carter and the Earl of Carnarvon. At least one royal tomb has yet to be found, that of Herihor of the 21st Dynasty.*

'There is a small [sic] and closeness in the tombs unpleasant to experience, and the discomfort is increased by the smoke and heat from the nude torches of the Arabs. The traveller should be provided with wax candles, which he will have occasion to use soon after entering the shaft of the tomb. For effect and for comfort, the visit to the tombs should be undertaken at night; and it is desirable to view the bold outline of the temples at the same time. The extent and grandeur of the architecture then make their full impression, while the faults and defects produced by time are concealed, and there is less risk of encountering interruption.

The entrances to the different tombs are represented in the Plate, at irregular distances, and without regard to position in different parts of the semi-circle. The tomb in which Champollion resided is pointed out [see pp. 130–31]; some remains of partition remained standing when I visited it, and, save for the close and unpleasant atmosphere, it was not an unsuitable place of domicile.

I returned to my abode completely tired with the exertion of the day, and looked forward with anxiety to the morrow, to enable me to reach the temple of Medinah Habou.' [pp. 124–25]

Captain Charles Francklin Head, *Eastern and Egyptian Scenery, Ruins, &c.,* 1833

*Captain Head was certainly right about the 'full impression' made by the temples at night (see p. 87).*

47 Captain Charles Francklin Head, *Approach to the tombs of the kings at Thebes, Biban-el-Muluk,* January 1830

# Thebes
## The Valley of the Kings

When Champollion's expedition arrived in the Valley of the Kings in 1829 they made their headquarters in the tomb of Ramesses IX (thought at the time to be that of Ramesses V). Champollion was accompanied by the Italian Egyptologist Ippolito Rosellini and a number of young draughtsmen and assistants. The two principals occupied the main rooms of the tomb and the others settled in around them.

Amongst the draughtsmen was Nestor L'Hôte, a young man of twenty-five who had been interested in Egypt since he was ten years old and who had met Champollion in 1827. He was an indefatigable worker, and many of his drawings were subsequently published in both Champollion's and Rosellini's great works. The strenuous conditions under which the party worked led to a deterioration in his health. He wrote home, in despair, 'God! Hieroglyphs are so boring and depressing! We are all sick of them!', and, 'I am like a man in the fire with only a quarter of an hour to live.' They spent June 1829 in the tomb in the Valley and then the main party moved down to Gourna, leaving Champollion and L'Hôte for a week to finish off some work. The conditions brought matters to a head, unrest spread, and some of the younger members decided to return to France, L'Hôte amongst them.

Champollion died in 1832 and L'Hôte returned to Egypt in 1838 to complete his drawings. On 23 July he wrote to another French archaeologist, Jean Latronne,

'I have taken up residence in the same tomb of Ramesses V where, eight years ago, I spent two months in the company of the illustrious and much lamented Champollion. This valley, which has reawoken in me the saddest yet most precious memories, has taken on an abandoned air, a touch of austere melancholy deeper than ever before. I have put my bed in the same place where his stood and my thoughts endeavour to resurrect his image, but it is impossible for me to invoke his immortal genius!'

L'Hôte's health did not long survive a third expedition, and he died in Paris in 1842, aged thirty-seven. Most of his vast output remains unpublished in the Louvre and Bibliothèque Nationale, Paris – but the task of sorting L'Hôte's papers had the effect of firing with enthusiasm his young kinsman, Auguste Mariette, who was to become a great Egyptologist in his turn.

The tomb of Ramesses IX was obviously a popular residence: this lithograph from a drawing by Owen Jones shows him and his companion Jules Goury relaxing with long pipes on low divans in the entrance to the tomb.

48 Owen Jones, *Interior of the tomb of Ramesses V [IX]*, 1832–33, from his *Views on the Nile*, 1843

# Thebes
## Tombs of the nobles

'Soon after noon day we arrived at a desert, which was the necropolis or city of the dead: the rock, excavated on its inclined plane, presents three sides of a square, with regular openings, behind which are double and triple galleries, which were used as burying places. I entered here on horseback, with Desaix, supposing that these gloomy retreats could only be the asylum of peace and silence; but scarcely were we immerged in the obscurity of these galleries, than we were assailed with javelins and stones, by enemies whom we could not distinguish, and this put an end to our observations.

[On a later visit the French drove out the tomb inhabitants.] I now began my researches, accompanied by some volunteers. I examined the grottoes that we had taken by assault: they were constructed without magnificence . . . If we had not observed tombs, and even some remains of mummies, we might be tempted to believe that these were the dwellings of the primitive inhabitants of Egypt . . . In proportion as the height of these grottoes encreases they become more richly decorated . . . The sculpture in all is incomparably more laboured and higher finished than any I had seen in the temples, . . . and I stood in astonishment at the high perfection of the art, and of its singular destiny, to be fixed in places devoted to silence and to obscurity . . . I thought it necessary to bring back with me some fragments of these bas-reliefs, as a specimen to others of what gave me so much surprise.'

Vivant Denon, *Travels*, 1803

'The people of Gournou [Gourna] are superior to any other Arabs in cunning and deceit, and the most independent of any in Egypt. They boast of being the last that the French had been able to subdue, and when subdued, they compelled them to pay the men whatever was asked for their labour; a fact which is corroborated by Baron Denon himself . . .

. . . There are no sepulchres in any part of the world like them . . . the entry or passage where the bodies are is roughly cut in the rocks, and the falling of the sand from the upper part or ceiling of the passages causes it to be nearly filled up . . . After getting through these passages, some of them two or three hundred yards long, you generally find a more commodious place, perhaps high enough to sit. But what a place of rest! Surrounded by bodies, by heaps of mummies in all directions; which, previous to my being accustomed to the sight, impressed me with horror . . . though fortunately, I am destitute of the sense of smelling, I could taste that the mummies were rather unpleasant to swallow. After the exertion of entering into such a place . . . nearly overcome, I sought a resting-place, found one, and contrived to sit; but when my weight bore on the body of an Egyptian, it crushed it like a band-box . . . I sunk altogether among the broken mummies, with a crash of bones, rags and wooden cases, which raised such a dust as kept me motionless for a quarter of an hour, waiting till it subsided again. I could not remove from the place, however, without increasing it, and every step I took I crushed a mummy in some part or other. Once I was conducted from such a place to another resembling it, through a passage of about twenty feet in length, and no wider than that a body could be forced through. It was choked with mummies, and I could not pass without putting my face in contact with that of some decayed Egyptian; but as the passage inclined downwards, my own weight helped me on: however, I could not avoid being covered with bones, legs, arms, and heads rolling from above . . . The purpose of my researches was to rob the Egyptians of their papyri; of which I found a few hidden in their breasts, under their arms, in the space above the knees, or on the legs, and covered by numerous folds of cloth, that envelop the mummy.'

Giovanni Belzoni, *Narrative*, 1820

*The tombs of the nobles differ from the royal tombs in having vivid scenes of everyday life painted on their walls.*

*The hills of the west bank are a warren of tombs, many of them simply galleries in which multiple burials were made in later periods. There were numerous finds to be made, not least the rolls of inscribed papyri, the Book of the Dead, often found swathed in the bandages between the legs of the mummy.*

49 Vivant Denon, *Tombs of the nobles at Thebes*, 1798, from his *Voyage*, 1802

133

# Armant

'. . . we went two leagues farther that night, till we got to Hermontes, where we slept, and for my share I was lodged in a temple. After dismounting, I profited by the small remains of day-light to take a figure of Typhon or Anubis. This was so often repeated in the temple where I took up my abode, that I concluded the whole was dedicated to him. He is represented standing up, with a belly like a pig, and breasts similar to those of the Egyptian women of the present day . . . At night I returned to my quarters, with my head confused by the profusion of objects which had passed before my eyes in so short a space of time.'

Vivant Denon, *Travels*, 1803

50 Dutertre, *The temple of Armant (Hermonthis) from the west*, 1798, from the *Description de l'Egypte*

*The temple was actually dedicated to the falcon-headed Montu, god of war; and it is from his name that the Greek name for the city, Hermonthes, derives. (A vast necropolis of the bulls sacred to him was found nearby and excavated in 1927 by Robert Mond and Walter B. Emery.) Little now remains, the temple having been largely dismantled – like Antinopolis (pp. 94–95) – to provide stone for building a large sugar factory nearby.*

51 Edward Hawker, *Ermenth or Hermonthis*, 5 February 1851

# Esna

*See also Pl. XX*

'. . . the Portico of the Temple of Latopolis, at Esneh, . . . [is] encumbered with dunghills and mean huts and hovels, which seemed to be placed there on purpose to set off the magnificence of this fine piece of antiquity. This edifice appears to me to be the most perfect in proportion, and the purest in execution of all the temples of Egypt, and is one of the finest monuments that antiquity can boast.'

Vivant Denon, *Travels*, 1803

52 Amelia B. Edwards, *Temple of Esneh*, 1874, from her *A Thousand Miles up the Nile*, 1877

'This is what we see – a little yard surrounded by mud-walls; at the farther end of the yard a dilapidated doorway; beyond the doorway, a strange-looking, stupendous mass of yellow limestone [in fact sandstone] masonry, long, and low, and level, and enormously massive . . . this proves to be the curved cornice of a mighty Temple – a Temple neither ruined nor defaced, but buried to the chin in the accumulated rubbish of a score of centuries . . . A low mud-parapet and a hand-rail reach from capital to capital. All beyond is vague, cavernous, mysterious – a great shadowy gulf, in the midst of which dim ghosts of many columns are darkly visible. From an opening between two of the capitals, a flight of brick steps leads down into a vast hall so far below the surface of the outer world, so gloomy, so awful, that it might be the portico of Hades.'

Amelia B. Edwards, *A Thousand Miles up the Nile*, 1877

136

The temple of Esna is mainly Roman in date (the latest hieroglyphic inscription is from the 3rd century AD); but such was the conservatism of Egyptian art and architecture that it has the same arrangement as Dendera (Ills. 30, 31), half a millennium earlier.

The pronaos was excavated by Mohammed Ali in 1842 for use as a gunpowder magazine, but fortunately, unlike the Parthenon, no ill befell it. The temple still stands far below the level of the modern town. On the roof, now no longer accessible, are many graffiti left by the French troops when they camped in the area, pursuing the Mamelukes south.

53 J. Jollois and R. E. Devilliers du Terrage, *Reconstruction of the interior of the portico of the temple of Esna (Latopolis) with a religious procession*, 1798, from the *Description de l'Egypte*

# El Kab

'This evening, August 15 [1817], we stopped at El Cab, the ancient Eleethias. These ruins are situated on the eastern bank of the Nile, not far from the river. The city has been inclosed by a wall of sun-burnt brick, thirty-seven feet thick; the place inclosed may be a mile square . . . At the back of the ruins, in the side of the Mockatem, are several sepulchral grottoes, two of which are well worthy of notice; the one is remarkable for a highly finished tablet of hieroglyphics, in intaglio; the other is a very interesting chamber [with detailed scenes of daily life] . . . We now visited a small temple situated in the plain, at a short distance to the N.W. The serpent Kneephis is said, by the French, to have been worshipped in this temple, though we could not observe any allusion to a serpent more than what is seen in every other temple; it consists of a single chamber surrounded by a gallery of square pillars.'

The Hon. Charles Leonard Irby and James Mangles, *Travels*, 1823

*El Kab was a very important city, capital of the 3rd Nome (one of 42 administrative areas). A few courses of sculptured blocks are all that remains of the temple within the massive mud-brick temenos wall. The tombs referred to, and seen being copied, are amongst the most important historical documents in Egypt. One of them, that of the Admiral Ahmose, son of Ebana, gives a very full account of the conflicts that hurled the Hyksos out of Egypt at the end of the 17th Dynasty (c. 1570 BC). The second tomb mentioned is that of Paheri, grandson of Ahmose. The little kiosk/temple out in the desert, more a wayside shrine, was built by Amenophis III (1417–1379 BC).*

54 *Right* Cécile, *Interior of a large tomb at El Kab*, 1798, from the *Description de l'Egypte*

55 *Opposite, above* George Alexander Hoskins, *Small shrine of Amenophis III, El Kab*, 1832–33

56 *Opposite, below* Dutertre, *The temple of El Kab*, 1798, from the *Description de l'Egypte*

# Edfu

*See also Pl. XXI*

'All those who could be spared [from the army chasing the Mamelukes] were ordered to proceed to Etfu; and I accompanied this party, in the hope of viewing at my leisure the sublime temple of Apollinopolis, the most beautiful of all Egypt, and, next to those of Thebes, the largest. Being built at a period when the arts and sciences had acquired all their splendour, the workmanship of every part is equally beautiful, the hieroglyphs are admirably executed, the figures more varied, and the architecture of a higher order than in the Theban edifices, the building of which must be referred to an earlier age . . .

Nothing can be more simply beautiful than these outlines, nothing more picturesque than the effect produced in the elevation, by the various dimensions belonging to each member of the harmonious whole. This superb edifice is seated on a rising ground, so as to overlook not only its immediate vicinity, but the whole valley . . .'

Vivant Denon, *Travels*, 1803

'Riding through lanes of huts, we came presently to an open space and a long flight of roughly-built steps in front of the Temple. At the top of these steps we were standing on the level of the modern village. At the bottom we saw the massive pavement that marked the level of the ancient city. From that level rose the pylons which even from afar off had looked so large. We now found that those stupendous towers not only soared to a height of about seventy-five feet above our heads, but plunged down to a depth of at least forty more beneath our feet.

Ten years ago nothing was visible of the great Temple of Edfoo save the tops of these pylons. The rest of the buildings was as much lost to sight as if the earth had opened and swallowed it. Its courtyards were choked with foul débris. Its sculptured chambers were buried under forty feet of soil. Its terraced roof was a maze of closely-packed huts, swarming with human beings, poultry, dogs, kine, asses, and vermin. Thanks to the enlightened liberality of the present ruler of Egypt, M. Mariette has been enabled to cleanse the Augaean stables.'

Amelia B. Edwards, *A Thousand Miles up the Nile*, 1877

58 Vivant Denon, *The temple of Edfu*, 1798, from his *Voyage*, 1802

*The temple complex was begun by Ptolemy II in 237 BC, the main temple finished by Ptolemy IV in 212, the hypostyle hall built under Ptolemy VIII, and the pylons then added and decorated by Ptolemy XII (father of Cleopatra) in 57 BC.*

*For David Roberts' comments on his drawings of Edfu, see Pl. XXI.*

57 *Opposite* David Roberts, *Edfu*, 23 November 1838

141

## Gebel Silsileh

'The next day I was more fortunate: we anchored opposite the large quarries of free-stone cut in the mountains, which form the banks of the Nile here on either side. This spot is called Gebel Silsilis, and is situated between Etfu and Ombos. The stone of these quarries being of an equal grain and uniform texture throughout, the blocks may be cut out of them as large as can be desired; and it is doubtless to the beauty and unalterability of this material, that we owe the vast size and fine preservation of the monuments which are our admiration at the present time, so many centuries after the date of their construction. From the immense excavations, and the quantity of fragments which may still be seen in these quarries, we may suppose that they were worked for some thousands of years; and they alone might have supplied the materials employed for the greater part of the monuments of Egypt.'

Vivant Denon, *Travels*, 1803

59 Balzac, *Rock-cut stelae at the landing place of the Silsileh quarries*, 1798, from the *Description de l'Egypte*

*Silsileh, 'the Mountain of the Chain', is where the Nile breaks through a rocky ridge. The quarries supplied the sandstone used for temple building throughout the New Kingdom, including most of the buildings of Thebes (limestone had been used in the Old Kingdom). Many master masons and high officials have inscribed records of their work here which are of paramount historical interest. The curious 'umbrella' pillar left after quarrying centuries ago, on the right of the illustration, still stands, and the few Nile steamers that call still tie up in front of the great 19th Dynasty stelae with royal inscriptions as the French are doing here.*

# Kom Ombo

*See also Pl. XXII*

'Here are the remains of two temples situated on a promontory of the Nile's eastern shore; the larger one, dedicated to the crocodile (as appears by the principal offerings being presented to a deity having the head of that animal) is situated at a short distance from the river, which it fronts. The smaller [the mamisi seen to the left in the reconstruction], to Isis, is close to the river side . . . The large temple consists of a portico of five columns in front, in three rows, though one at each of the outer angles is fallen. The cornice, only two parts of which are perfect, is ornamented with four winged globes [sun disks].'

The Hon. Charles Leonard Irby and James Mangles, *Travels*, 1823

*Amelia Edwards feared that Kom Ombo would disappear forever, 'for the Nile is gradually sapping the bank, and carrying away piecemeal from below what the desert has buried from above'. Fortunately her pessimism was ill-founded, and the temple has been restored. Unique in having a dual dedication, to Horus (hawk-headed) and Sobek (crocodile-headed), it is divided along its axis – hence the two entrances – by an invisible line on either side of which the ritual of the two gods proceeded in·parallel. Much of the original bright colour remains on its superb Ptolemaic capitals.*

60 J. Jollois and R. E. Devilliers du Terrage, *Reconstruction view of the double temple at Kom Ombo with the entrance pylon on the right and mamisi on the left*, 1798, from the *Description de l'Egypte*

61 Charles Barry, *Koum Ombos*, 1819

# Aswan

'The green island of Elephantine, which is about a mile in length, lies opposite Assouan and divides the Nile in two channels. The Libyan and Arabian deserts – smooth amber sand-slopes on the one hand; rugged granite cliffs on the other – come down to the brink on either side. On the Libyan shore a Sheykh's tomb, on the Arabian shore a bold fragment of Moorish architecture with ruined arches open to the sky, crown two opposing heights, and keep watch over the gate of the Cataract. Just under the Moorish ruin, and separated from the river by a slip of sandy beach, lies Assouan.'

Amelia B. Edwards, *A Thousand Miles up the Nile*, 1877

62 Edward Lear, *Assouan*, 9 February 1854 (detail)

*The sheik's tomb, a small white domed building seen in the distance in Edward Lear's sketch, dominated the skyline of Aswan for more than a hundred years. Now, a little further south, it has a domed companion – the mausoleum of the Aga Khan, spiritual leader of the Ismaili Muslims, who died in 1957.*

146

# Aswan quarries

'. . . we met in our way with the quarries in the granite rocks, whence the blocks were taken which formed the material of the colossal statues, that have been the object of admiration to so many ages, and the ruins of which still strike us with astonishment. It seemed as if the framers wished to preserve the memorial of the masses that have produced these blocks, by leaving on the place hieroglyphical inscriptions, that perhaps record the event. The operation by which these blocks were detached, must have been nearly the same as is employed in the present times, that is to say, a cleft is first cut out, and then the whole mass is split off by means of wedges of different sizes, all struck in at one time. The marks of these first operations are preserved so fresh in the unalterable material, that to look at them one would suspect that the work had been interrupted only yesterday. I took a sketch of them.'

Vivant Denon, *Travels*, 1803

*Denon was perfectly correct in both his guesses. The rocks around Aswan preserve many historic inscriptions of masons and of Egyptian expeditions down into Kush (Nubia, the Sudan). All the obelisks were cut from the Aswan quarries as single shafts; one that broke because of a flaw in the granite still lies there, the 'unfinished obelisk', calculated to weigh about one thousand tons. Out in the desert there are other unfinished pieces – a colossal statue and a sarcophagus.*

63 Vivant Denon, *Quarries at Aswan*, 1798, from his *Voyage*, 1802

# Elephantine

'About the middle of the island is situated the small Temple, of which only one column, 5 square pilasters and part of the flank wall of the Cella now remain... The whole is of rough construction...'

Charles Barry, diary, 12 December 1818

*Denon also drew this temple, one of the smaller examples of several on the island, from virtually the same spot. He, however, had a different opinion from Barry since he mentions the 'hieroglyphs in relief, very well cut, and in good preservation'. He goes on, 'I copied a whole side of the inner figures ... the corresponding side appears to be nearly a repetition of the same ... The view of the whole of this small edifice will give an idea of its importance, and high state of preservation.' When Champollion was in Egypt in 1828–29 he could only sadly point out to Mohammed Ali's chief dragoman that this small temple and another on Elephantine had but recently disappeared.*

64 Charles Barry, *Temple in the island of Elephantina near the first Cataracts. Upper Egypt*, 1818

148

# Philae

*See also Pls. XXIV–XXVI*

'The prospect of the island of Philoe and its ruins is truly magnificent, particularly at some distance, though it is extremely barren [Pl. XXIV]. It is surrounded by rocks of granite in all directions, forming part of the mainland, and part of other islands. The style of the hieroglyphics proves, that the edifice on it is of the last era of the Egyptian nation: in my opinion, of the time of the Ptolemies . . . There are other proofs that this temple is a more modern structure, formed of the materials of an older edifice. In one of the columns, opposite the gate in the portico which leads to the sanctuary, there is in the centre a stone, sculptured with hieroglyphics inverted; and another stone of this kind is to be seen in the same column on the west side, near the ground. . . . I cannot help observing, that this island is the most superb group of ruins I have ever beheld together in so small a space of ground. The whole island, which is not more than a thousand feet in length, and less than five hundred in breadth, is richly covered with ruins; and being detached from the other barren islands which surround it at some distance, has a very superb appearance.'

Giovanni Belzoni, *Narrative*, 1820

65 *Below* Edward William Cooke, *Philae, Nubia*, 21 December 1874

66 *Opposite* L. M. A. Linant de Bellefonds, *Great Temple of Isis, Philae, seen from the southern tip of the island*

*Philae, with its temple of Isis and kiosk built by the emperor Trajan, is one of the most numinous places in Egypt, and certainly the most illustrated. Flooded by the first Aswan Dam after 1902, and doomed by the new High Dam, the buildings were dismantled and re-erected on a nearby island (admittedly slightly smaller) above the water level, and formally reopened in 1980.*

EW COOKE . RA .

'The next day was the finest to me of my whole travels: I possessed seven or eight monuments in the space of six hundred yards, and could examine them quite at my ease, for I had not by my side any of those impatient companions who always think they have seen enough, and are constantly pressing you to go to some other object, nor had I in my ears the beating of drums as a signal to muster, or to march, nor Arabs nor peasants to torment me; I was alone in full leisure, and could make my drawings without interruption. This was my sixth visit to Philae; the five first I had employed in taking views of the shores of the vicinity.'

Vivant Denon, *Travels*, 1803

*In both pictures the Ptolemaic temple of Isis is on the left and Trajan's Kiosk on the right (see Pl. XXVI and Ill. 67). Cooke's drawing also shows the small pavilion perched on the southern tip of the island, built in the 4th century BC by Nectanebo II, the last native pharaoh. Between it and the first pylon is the colonnade built by Augustus, the right-hand side of which was never finished. This is seen in Linant's view; in the foreground are the ruins of the temple of Arsenuphis, its internal carvings exposed. The pylon is decorated with the traditional scene of pharaoh slaying prisoners and making offerings to gods. The pharaoh here, as at Edfu, is Ptolemy XII, father of Cleopatra.*

151

XXIII A.C.T.E. Prisse d'Avennes, *A Nubian girl beside ruins on the Nile*

*A charming capriccio shows a Nubian girl standing beside an ancient Egyptian inscribed block and a Roman grave stone near a cataract. Many painters were much taken by the artlessness of the Nubians, especially the scantily clothed women. Roberts made several studies of them, as individuals, in a group, or to set as a scale beside his Nubian monuments. The inscription on the tomb stone purports to record a soldier, Aemilius Gaius, of the XXIV Legion, just one of the many who died in the service of Rome – but that legion never served in Egypt!*

XXIV David Roberts, *General View of the Island of Philae, Nubia, Nov 14th 1838*, from *Egypt and Nubia*, 1846–50

'The prospect extends over an assemblage of temples, and the islet, amidst rich verdure, is strewn with marble wrought into every beautiful form known to ancient art; over prostrate columns palms are waving, mingled with the foliage and blossoms of the acacia. Around the island flows the clear, bright river, and on its brink lies the old Temple of Osiris, now called Pharaoh's Bed; beyond the river green patches dispute the surface with the drifts of desert sands, palms, rocks, and villages; beyond all, and darkly encircling this paradise, rises the rugged chain of Hemeceuta, or Golden Mountains.

The Island of Philae was esteemed the most sacred place in the dominions of Egypt . . .'

William Brockedon, note to David Roberts, *Egypt and Nubia*, 1846–50

*The view is taken from the now submerged island of Biga. The entrance to the temple on Philae is via the great colonnade on the right and through the first pylon (centre, from in front of which Belzoni retrieved the Philae obelisk, now at Kingston Lacy, Dorset). In the background is 'Pharaoh's Bed'. Between the first and second pylons is the mamisi, or birth-house of Horus. The main temple of Isis with its hypostyle hall (XXV) and sanctuary extends beyond the second pylon.*

XXV David Roberts, *View under the Grand Portico, Philae*, from *Egypt and Nubia*, 1846–50

*Roberts was extremely fond of views taken under a shady colonnade, such as this in the temple of Isis, and made similar studies in most of the major Egyptian temples.*

XXVI David Roberts, *The Hypaethral Temple at Philae called the Bed of Pharaoh*, from *Egypt and Nubia*, 1846–50

'. . . We skirt the steep banks, and pass close under the beautiful little roofless Temple commonly known as Pharaoh's Bed – that Temple which has been so often painted, so often photographed, that every stone of it, and the platform on which it stands, and the tufted palms that cluster round about it, have been since childhood as familiar to our mind's eye as the Sphinx or the Pyramids.'

Amelia B. Edwards, *A Thousand Miles up the Nile*, 1877

*'Pharaoh's Bed', or Trajan's Kiosk, is almost the epitome of Egyptian architecture, yet, strangely, it is strictly Romano–Egyptian, begun by the emperor Trajan (AD 98–117) and left unfinished.*

General View of the Island of Philæ, Nubia. Nov. 19th 1838. David Roberts R.A.

XXVII     Colossus in front of Temple of Wady Saboua - Nubia.

XXVIII

XXIX

XXX

'Immediately in front of the propylon originally stood two fine colossal figures [of Ramesses II] . . . Both these statues have fallen, but our Artist has placed one standing, to show the symmetry of its form.'

William Brockedon, note to David Roberts, *Egypt and Nubia*, 1855–56 ed.

XXVII David Roberts, *Colossus in front of Temple of Wady Saboua, Nubia*, from *Egypt and Nubia*, 1846–50

For Wadi es Sebua see p. 171

'Early in the morning of the 1st August we went to the temple in high spirits, at the idea of entering a newly discovered place. We endeavoured as much as we could to enlarge the entrance; but our crew did not accompany us as usual . . . The fact was, they had promised to the Cacheffs to play some trick to interrupt our proceedings, in case we should come to the door. But even all this would not do. We soon made the passage wider, and entered the finest and most extensive excavation in Nubia . . .

From what we could perceive at the first view, it was evidently a very large place; but our astonishment increased, when we found it to be one of the most magnificent of temples, enriched with beautiful intaglios, painting, colossal figures, &c. . . . The heat was so great in the interior of the temple, that it scarcely permitted us to take any drawings, as the perspiration from our hands soon rendered the paper quite wet. Accordingly, we left this operation to succeeding travellers, who may set about it with more convenience than we could, as the place will become cooler.'

Giovanni Belzoni, *Narrative*, 1820

XXVIII Giovanni Belzoni, *Exterior View of the Two Temples at Ybsambul*, 1820

XXIX Giovanni Belzoni, *View of the Interior of the Temple of Ybsombul in Nubia. Opened by G. Belzoni, 1818* [*i.e. 1817*], 1820

XXX L.M.A. Linant de Bellefonds, *Excavation of the Great Temple of Ramesses II at Abu Simbel*, February 1819

*Belzoni's distant view shows the vast drift of sand between the Great Temple of Ramesses II and the Small Temple which obscured the figures of the former and blocked its entrance. Belzoni, accompanied by Irby, Mangles, and Henry Beechey, penetrated to the interior on 1 August 1817 (see p. 174). In 1818–19 Henry Salt continued the clearance, an enormous task beset with problems by the constantly encroaching sand, here seen held back beside the entrance by a palisade of palm tree trunks. It was at this point that it became apparent that the four colossi were seated, not standing.*

67 Owen Jones, *Landing Place, Philoe, Upper Egypt*, 1832–33

'As the boat glides nearer between glistening boulders, those sculptured towers rise higher and ever higher against the sky. They show no sign of ruin or of age. All looks solid, stately, perfect. One forgets for the moment that anything is changed. If a sound of antique chanting were to be borne along the quiet air – if a procession of white-robed priests bearing aloft the veiled ark of the God, were to come sweeping round between the palms and the pylons – we should not think it strange.'

Amelia B. Edwards, *A Thousand Miles up the Nile*, 1877

*Once it was a cause of some concern to historians and Egyptologists that Herodotus, when he visited Aswan in the 5th century BC, did not mention Philae. It was thought that the dedications and temples must be earlier than his visit. We now know that there was nothing on the island at the time and that the majority of the buildings are of the Ptolemaic period.*

*One of the last Egyptian temples to be built, Philae was the last in which the old religion continued to be practised. The Byzantine emperor Justinian finally closed the temple in the 6th century AD.*

# Debod

'Friday, August 8 [1817]. At noon we inspected the temple of Daboude; it is situated about two hundred yards from the river side, and is altogether unfinished. The approach is by three portals, after which comes the temple, consisting of a portico, composed of four columns in front, and a wall of intercolumniation reaching half way up the pillars. Within this there are two chambers and a sanctuary; the latter contains two handsome monolithe cages of red granite, between six and seven feet high, and about four feet broad; these are the only objects of interest which the temple contains.'

The Hon. Charles Leonard Irby and James Mangles, *Travels*, 1823

'. . . arrived at Debodé about 1 oclock where we met the whole of Mr Salts Party busily engaged at the Temple. . . .'

Charles Barry, diary, 17 December 1818

68 David Roberts, *Temple at Wady Dabod, Nubia,* from *Egypt and Nubia*, 1846–50

*This little temple is of Graeco–Roman date. As part of the Save the Monuments of Nubia campaign the Egyptian Government allowed it to be dismantled and taken to Madrid, where it is now rebuilt on a cliff with an artificial channel before it simulating its original location.*

# Kertassi

'It stands unrelieved against the deep blue of the sky in a blaze of sunshine, and appears as if the hand of the destroyer had only just been stayed. From the total want of moisture, the very stones when struck ring like a bell.'
David Roberts, journal, quoted in *Egypt and Nubia*, 1846–50

*This graceful little pavilion with its Hathor-headed capitals stood on a knoll overlooking the Nile on the west bank. Reminiscent of Trajan's Kiosk at Philae (Ill. 67), it was much sketched by passing travellers. It has now been re-erected on a site near the new High Dam.*

69 John Gardner Wilkinson, *Kertassi kiosk*, ?1821

164

'At Tafah there are two little temples; one in picturesque ruin, one quite perfect, and now used as a stable . . . Tafah is charmingly placed; and the seven miles which divide it from Kalabsheh – once, no doubt, the scene of a cataract – are perhaps the most picturesque on this side of Wady Halfeh.'

Amelia B. Edwards, *A Thousand Miles up the Nile*, 1877

# Tafa

Both the small temples at Tafa were built in the reign of the emperor Augustus (27 BC–AD 14). The southern one had been reduced to a 'picturesque ruin' about 1870 but the other, 'quite perfect', survived on the site until the great rescue campaign in Nubia began in the 1960s. In 1969 it was presented by Egypt to the Netherlands as a mark of appreciation of that country's help in the campaign, and ten years later its 657 sandstone blocks were re-erected in the Rijksmuseum van Oudheden at Leiden.

70 Edward Hawker, *Tafa*, January 1851

165

# Kalabsha

*This temple, which stood in the ancient city of Talmis, seems to have been founded under Amenophis II in the 18th Dynasty, but the structure seen by the travellers dated from the reign of Augustus. It was dedicated to the god Mandulis, a Nubian version of Osiris. Its most important feature is the inscription in Greek (which Irby and Mangles noted but did not record) of Silko, king of the Nobatae in the mid-6th century AD, which tells how he fought against the nomadic Blemmyes. Not long afterwards Christianity was finally established throughout Nubia.*

*The temple was the second largest in Nubia after Abu Simbel. During the rescue operations it was dismantled by West German engineers and stored as a series of numbered blocks for some years on Elephantine Island. It has now been re-erected on a promontory close to the south side of the High Dam on the west bank overlooking Lake Nasser.*

'This evening we arrived at Kalapshe, and as we had to wait some time while our janissary was buying provisions, we went up to inspect the temple, though we had agreed to visit the antiquities in general as we returned from the second cataract. The ruins of this edifice are large and magnificent, but it has never been finished: it consists of a large peristyle hall, (most of the columns of which have fallen, and many are unfinished), two chambers, and a sanctuary. The exterior walls are smooth, the sculpture not having even been commenced, and in the interior it is not finished, there being in no instance either stucco or painting. There has been first a quay on the river's side, and then a flight of steps as an approach to the temple. We reserved the measurements, &c. till our return: the outer hall had several Greek inscriptions in it, some of them in tolerable perfection.'

The Hon. Charles Leonard Irby and James Mangles, *Travels*, 1823

*Irby and Mangles never did get their measurements, for when they returned from Abu Simbel with Belzoni the natives at Kalabsha were most unfriendly: 'on shoving off, they pelted us with stones; we fired a musket over their heads, to shew them that we had ammunition though we did not choose to use it unless there was real occasion'.*

'But if the decorative work in the presence-chamber of the Caesars was anything like the decorative work in the Temple of Kalabsheh, then the taste thereof was of the vilest. Such a masquerade of deities; such striped and spotted and cross-barred robes; such outrageous head-dresses; such crude and violent colouring, we have never seen the like of. As for the goddesses, they are gaudier than the dancing damsels of Luxor; while the kings balance on their heads diadems compounded of horns, moons, birds, balls, beetles, lotus-blossoms, asps, vases, and feathers. The Temple, however, is conceived on a grand scale. It is the Karnak of Nubia. But it is a Karnak that has evidently been visited by a shock of earthquake far more severe than that which shook the mighty pillars of the Hypostyle Hall and flung down the obelisk of Hatasu [Hatshepsut]. From the river, it looks like a huge fortress; but seen from the threshold of the main gateway, it is a wilderness of ruin. Fallen blocks, pillars, capitals, entablatures, lie so extravagantly piled, that there is not one spot in all those halls and courtyards upon which it is possible to set one's foot on the level of the original pavement.'

Amelia B. Edwards, *A Thousand Miles up the Nile*, 1877

71 Charles Barry, *Kalaptchie*, December 1818

167

# Dendur

'At Dendoor, when the sun is setting and a delicious gloom is stealing up the valley, we visit a tiny Temple on the western bank. It stands out above the river surrounded by a wall of enclosure, and consists of a single pylon, a portico, two little chambers, and a sanctuary. The whole thing is like an exquisite toy, so covered with sculptures, so smooth, so new-looking, so admirably built. Seeing them half by sunset, half by dusk, it matters not that these delicately-wrought bas-reliefs are of the Decadence school [i.e. Roman date]. The rosy half-light of an Egyptian after-glow covers a multitude of sins, and steeps the whole in an atmosphere of romance.'

Amelia B. Edwards, *A Thousand Miles up the Nile*, 1877

72 Edward Hawker, *Dendour*, 18 January 1851

*Like Philae, Dendur was flooded for much of the year after the building of the first Aswan Dam, and would have been destroyed by the High Dam. It was therefore dismantled in 1963 by the Egyptian Department of Antiquities and its friable sandstone blocks, carefully numbered and marked, were floated on barges down the Nile, to be stored on Elephantine Island for the next five years. In 1965 the temple was offered by Egypt to the United States to mark American financial aid in the Save Nubia campaign, and after much hard work it was re-erected in the specially designed Sackler Wing of the Metropolitan Museum of Art, New York.*

73 David Roberts, *Excavated Temple of Gyrshe, Nubia,* from *Egypt and Nubia,* 1855–56 ed.

74 Frederick Catherwood, *Guerfeh Hassan, Nubia,* painted in 1835 from a drawing made in 1824

'. . . the Temple [is] approached through the ruins of a built-out portico and an avenue of battered colossi. It is a gloomy place within – an inferior edition, so to say, of the Great Temple of Aboo Simbel; and of the same date. It consists of a first hall supported by Osiride pillars, a second and smaller hall with square columns; a smoke-blackened sanctuary; and two side-chambers. The Osiride colossi, which stand 20 feet high without the entablature over their heads or the pedestal under their feet, are thick-set, bow-legged, and mis-shapen. Their faces would seem to have been painted black originally; while those of the avenue outside have distinctly Ethiopian features. One seems to detect here, as at Derr and Wady Sabooah, the work of provincial sculptors . . .'

Amelia B. Edwards, *A Thousand Miles up the Nile,* 1877

# Gerf Hussain

*This rock-cut temple built by Ramesses II has suffered from being compared to its larger contemporary, Abu Simbel (Ills. 79, 80), but it is still an impressive edifice.*

# Dakka

*See also Pl. XXVII*

'In the afternoon of the next day we arrived at Dakka . . . The temple stands about a hundred yards from the river, and has a very elegant appearance. There are no hieroglyphics on the outside wall, but the interior is adorned with beautiful figures in basso relievo: it has a pronaos, an adytum, and a cella. On the west side of the adytum is a small staircase that leads to the top of the temple; and on the east a small chamber with figures uncommonly well executed: the walls of the cella are well covered with religious processions . . . The temple faces the north, and at the distance of forty-eight feet is a propylaeon, with the gateway facing the entrance to the pronaos. The isolated situation of this edifice renders it still more graceful to the eyes of the traveller, as it is entirely free from any other building near it.'

Giovanni Belzoni, *Narrative*, 1820

75 Edward Lane, *Temple of Dakka, c. 1827*

'Of the Temple I will only say that, as masonry, it is better put together than any work of the XVIIIth or XIXth Dynasties with which I am acquainted. The sculptures, however, are atrocious. Such mis-shapen hieroglyphs; such dumpy, smirking goddesses; such clownish kings in such preposterous head-dresses, we have never seen till now. The whole thing, in short, as regards sculpturesque style, is the Ptolemaic out-Ptolemied.'

Amelia B. Edwards, *A Thousand Miles up the Nile*, 1877

*Obviously Amelia Edwards and Belzoni did not see eye to eye regarding the reliefs at Dakka. The temple is an 18th Dynasty foundation but was largely rebuilt in Ptolemaic and Roman times. It was in the latter period that the sanctuary and pylon were added. The reliefs of the sanctuary are particularly clumsy and it is probably those that drew so strong a reaction from Amelia Edwards. Dakka has now been moved to a site of safety beside Wadi es Sebua.*

'. . . we come one afternoon to Wady Sabooah, where there is a solitary Temple drowned in sand. It was approached once by an avenue of sphinxes and standing colossi, now shattered and buried. The roof of the pronaos, if ever it was roofed, is gone. The inner halls and the sanctuary – all excavated in the rock – are choked and impassable. Only the propylon stands clear of sand; and that, massive as it is, looks as if one touch of a battering-ram would bring it to the ground.'

Amelia B. Edwards, *A Thousand Miles up the Nile*, 1877

# Wadi es Sebua

*See also Pl. XXVII*

76 Frederick Catherwood, *Temple of Sabooa, Nubia*, 10 February 1824

*Wadi es Sebua is a fine temple built by Ramesses II in honour of Amun, Ra-Herakhti and himself. It was converted into a church by the early Christians, who plastered over many of the reliefs and added frescoes. In the niche at the rear of the sanctuary sit three mutilated statues, Ramesses himself in the centre flanked by his companion gods. On the walls on either side of the niche he was shown as pharaoh offering flowers to himself as a god. However, above his mutilated statue the Christians painted a fresco of St Peter with the key of heaven – to whom Ramesses now offers flowers.*

*In a joint project by Egyptian, French and Swiss engineers the temple was dismantled and moved to higher ground nearby.*

# Amada

'. . . arrived at Amada on the opposite side of the River in about 1½ hours and immediately repaired to the Temple – the plan of it is different from any other we have yet seen – it at present consists first of a small porch or entrance, in front the Pronaos which consists of 12 pilasters and 4 columns, the former appearing 4 in front and 3 in depth and the latter in a row at the back of them immediately in front of the Cella. It is roofed by long thick stones lying upon the frieze above the pilasters and columns . . .'

Charles Barry, diary, 12 January 1819

*Amada was erected under Tuthmosis III and Amenophis II in the 15th century BC. The Copts later built in and on the temple, and covered the fine reliefs with stucco and paint – thus unintentionally preserving much of the original colouring. The temple's rescue from the rising waters of Lake Nasser therefore presented special problems: French engineers boldly lifted it as a single mass (weighing some 800 tons) and moved it by rail to a safer site.*

77 Charles Barry, *Amada in Nubia*, January 1819

'The Temple here, though dating from the reign of Rameses II., is of rude design and indifferent execution. Partly constructed, partly excavated, it is approached by a forecourt, the roof of which, now gone, was supported by eight square columns. Of these columns only the bases remain. Four massive piers against which once stood four colossi, upheld the roof of the portico and gave admission by three entrances to the rock-cut chambers beyond. That portico is now roofless. Nothing is left of the colossi but their feet. All is ruin; and ruin without beauty.'

Amelia B. Edwards, *A Thousand Miles up the Nile*, 1877

# Derr

*The interior of the rock-cut temple had a very fine series of reliefs relating to the Nubian campaigns of Ramesses II. As at Abu Simbel (Ill. 80), there were four seated gods in the sanctuary, but they, like the colossi outside, have been destroyed down to their feet. The structure is very much damaged but it was saved from being flooded by being removed to a new site beside the temple of Amada.*

78 Edward Lear, *Derr*, 11 February 1867

# Abu Simbel

*See also Pls. XXVIII–XXX*

'The temple is situated on the side of the Nile, about two or three hundred yards from its western bank [Pl. XXVIII]; it stands upon an elevation, and its base is considerably above the level of the river: it is excavated in the mountain, and its front presents a flat surface of upwards of sixty feet in height, above the summit of the sand immediately above the door, but not as much as forty on the north side, and a little more on the south; the breadth is one hundred and seventeen feet . . . Before the front of the temple are four sitting colossal figures cut out of the solid mountain, chairs and all . . . They are in a sitting posture, above sixty feet high, and the two which are partly uncovered, are sculptured in the best style of Egyptian art; and are in a much higher state of preservation than any colossal statues remaining in Egypt. They are uncovered at present only as far as the breast; before [our] recent excavations, one of the faces was alone partly visible, and part of the head-dress of the other remaining two . . .

The interior of this temple is a work not inferior to any excavation in Egypt or Nubia, not even excepting the Tombs of the Kings [the tomb of Seti I was not discovered until three months later]; indeed the effect produced on first encountering it, may be considered as more striking than any which those can afford; the loftiness of the cieling, the imposing height of the square pillars, and of the erect colossal statues attached to them, full thirty feet high . . . all contribute to render the interior of this temple not less admirable than its splendid exterior.

[Irby, Mangles and Henry Beechey, led by Belzoni, had opened the temple on 1 August 1817, under strenuous conditions, which they described in a note.] The time employed in clearing away the sand was 22 days; the first 5 the work was done by 100 natives paid by Henry Salt Esqr. (H.B.M. Consul Genl. in Egypt) the last 17 days only the four persons above mentioned, assisted by a Turkish soldier and a Greek servant laboured at the undertaking (the natives having refused further assistance) viz. 10 hours each day, from daylight till 8 in the morning, from 2 (when the Mountain afforded them a Shade) till dusk: the depth of the sand dug down was about 50 feet. The average height of the Ther. in the shade during the operations was 112° of Fahrenheit.

During the last 5 days their food consisted of only doura and water, the natives having cut off their supplies to prevent them from accomplishing their object.'

The Hon. Charles Leonard Irby and James Mangles, *Travels*, 1823

*The Great Temple had only been discovered four years earlier, when it was literally stumbled upon by the Swiss explorer J. L. Burckhardt (1784–1817). The smaller temple was well known to the local people, who used it as a refuge when one of their frequent feuds broke out. Burckhardt visited it in 1813; on leaving he strayed away onto the drift between the temples (Pl. XXVIII) and found a huge carved head protruding from the sand.*

*It must have been galling for the party to have to leave their splendid discovery after only three days, on 4 August. Henry Salt himself came later to investigate Belzoni's find and to carry out further excavations and clearance of the sand (Pl. XXX).*

79 Joseph Bonomi, *Façade of the Great Temple, Abu Simbel,* ?1829 (detail)

80 David Roberts, *The Hypostyle Hall of the Great Temple of Abu Simbel*

'A solemn twilight reigned in the first hall, beyond which all was dark. Eight colossi . . . stand ranged down the centre, bearing the mountain on their heads. Their height is twenty-five feet. With hands crossed on their breasts, they clasp the flail and crook; emblems of majesty and dominion. It is the attitude of Osiris, but the face is the face of Rameses II.'

Amelia B. Edwards, *A Thousand Miles up the Nile*, 1877

*Less than a century after Amelia Edwards' visit the temples of Abu Simbel became the focal point of the Save the Monuments of Nubia campaign launched by UNESCO. They had to be cut from their mountain backing, lifted up 62 metres (200 feet), and moved to another location 200 metres (700 feet) from their original site, where a new mountain was created to preserve their effect. The whole enterprise was carried out by an international team of technicians over a period of four and a half years at a cost of around £17 million.*

176

One of the consequences of the rediscovery of ancient Egypt was that the country and its culture entered the repertoire of history painters. In the Neoclassical period there was already keen interest in subjects drawn from Greek and Roman history, depicted with settings and costumes of the greatest possible accuracy, and in the 19th century this desire to recapture the appearance of bygone times increased. Be it ancient Assyria or the age of Louis XIV, modern men sought to experience what life was like in the past – to feel with a *frisson*, 'I was there!' Egypt enjoyed great popularity for its biblical associations, which remained a fertile source of themes. Subjects from non-biblical history were rarer. A third area for painters to explore was everyday life in ancient Egypt, and they did so increasingly as the century progressed.

When in 1827 Abel de Pujol (1787–1861) painted the ceiling of one of the galleries in the Paris Louvre where some of the newly acquired Egyptian antiquities were to be displayed, the subject was *Egypt saved by Joseph* and the setting a Ptolemaic temple portico based on Philae. The short-lived Adrien Guignet (1816–54) painted a *Flight into Egypt* and *Joseph explaining the Dreams of Pharaoh*, but he also chose a non-biblical subject: against the background of a pyramid and a seated colossus, he shows the moment in 525 BC when the invading Persian king Cambyses has conquered and is about to execute the Saite king Psammetichus III.

That doyen of topographical artists on the Nile, David Roberts, was already interested in Egypt long before his visit in 1838–39. In 1829 he painted for the collector Lord Northwick *The Departure of the Israelites*, having chosen the topic, he explained, 'as a Vehicle for introducing that grand although simple style of architecture – the Egyptian'. What he thought of as the style of Egyptian architecture was late, Ptolemaic or Graeco-Roman – a preference which was shared not only by Denon (p. 140) but by most 19th-century artists and travellers. In its complex structures and details and its megalomaniac quality the picture is much closer to the manner of the visionary painter John Martin than to Roberts' clean and unfussy mature style [XXI].

Roughly contemporary with Roberts' large canvas is a little watercolour by William West (1801–69), of the Bristol School, which exemplifies a different painterly approach to ancient Egypt: the capriccio incorporating aspects of several different monuments, which seemed accurate to those who did not know the elements, and amusing to those who did.

The great illustrated books which gradually came out provided a rich lode of material for artists: first the *Description de l'Egypte* (1809), then Rosellini's *Monumenti dell'Egitto* (1832–44), followed by Wilkinson's *Manners and Customs of the Ancient Egyptians* (1837), Roberts'

# Afterword: the Imaginative Response

Abel de Pujol, *Egypt saved by Joseph*, 1827; ceiling of Room C of the Egyptian Antiquities Department, Louvre, Paris

David Roberts, *The Departure of the Israelites*, 1829

William West, *Ruins on the Nile*, a capriccio, *c.* 1829

Jean Léon Gérôme, *Sword-Dance*

After Hans Makart
*Ancient Egyptian Dancing Girl*, from Georg Ebers, *Egypt*, 1881

*Egypt and Nubia* (1846–50), Lepsius's *Denkmäler* (1849–59) and Prisse d'Avennes' *Histoire de l'Art Egyptien* (1858–77). In addition, several historical painters actually visited Egypt. Jean-Léon Gérôme (1824–1904) travelled in the Near East as a young man, and returned to Paris to extend the manner of his teacher Delaroche to more exotic subjects, setting an antique sword-dance against the Hathor-headed columns of the birth-house at Philae.

Another source of information was the German Egyptologist Georg M. Ebers (1837–98), who was himself a popularizer of ancient Egypt. In addition to his scholarly publications, he was known as a storyteller and writer of historical novels: his *Ägyptische Königstochter* (*An Egyptian Princess*) was still in print thirty years after his death, had been translated into sixteen languages and sold some 400,000 copies. His popular book on Egypt, *Ägypten in Wort und Bild*, was translated into French and English (*Egypt*, 1881); it introduced a wide audience to the country and its antiquities, and – with the added spice of historical paintings – its ancient culture.

Ebers' *Egyptian Princess* provided a pictorial subject for the glamorous Austrian *salon* painter Hans Makart (1840–84), who with other artist friends, including the portraitist Franz von Lenbach, spent the winter of 1875–76 in Cairo, occupying the old Mameluke palace of the Khedive. He was seduced by Egypt: painting *The Death of Cleopatra*, which he had previously treated in a generalized Baroque manner, he introduced Egyptian details, and he also invented genre scenes with an Egyptian flavour, such as a lavish *Hunt on the Nile* and an alluring *Ancient Egyptian Dancing Girl*.

The latter is included among the illustrations in Ebers' *Egypt*, which also featured a quite improbable picture by Wilhelm Gentz (1822–90) of a chained girl about to be sacrificed to the Nile, a romantic *Voyage to the Nekropolis* by the Warsaw-born Berlin artist Ludwig Burger (1825–84), and a *Finding of Moses* – that ever-popular subject – painted in 1878 by Ferdinand Keller (1842–1922), with a few token sphinxes and hieroglyphs in what is otherwise a Rococo composition. The frontispiece to Ebers' first volume is Sir Edward Poynter's *Israel in Egypt*, of which more later.

The artist featured most extensively by Ebers is Alma Tadema. He was a great friend of the author, but earned his prominence by being the most prolific and skilled of all who worked in his field: his biographer Swanson aptly called him 'the painter of the Victorian vision of the ancient world'. Sir Lawrence Alma Tadema (1836–1912) was born in the Netherlands, and though thought of as British did not move to England until he was thirty-four. He studied at the Antwerp Academy, where he came under the influence of Louis Delaye, the professor of archaeology, and painted his first Egyptian subject in

1859 – *The Sad Father*, which was also the first of a series
of pictures he was to paint on the theme of the death of
the firstborn. In 1862 he visited London, where he was
impressed not only by the Elgin Marbles but by the
Egyptian antiquities in the British Museum, returning
home to paint *Pastimes in Ancient Egypt: 3,000 Years Ago*,
which won the Gold Medal at the Paris Salon of 1864.
Much of the detail must have been gleaned from
architectural studies published by Champollion and
others; the source for the harpists could be either
Wilkinson's *Manners and Customs* or Prisse d'Avennes'
*Histoire de l'Art Egyptien*, both of which reproduce in
bright colour the harpists and their instruments from the
tomb of Ramesses III. Several other pictures with Egyptian
themes followed in the late 1860s, some of which were
illustrated in Ebers' *Egypt*. They include *An Egyptian at
his Doorway in Memphis* (1865), *The Mummy: Roman
Period: Egyptians lamenting their Dead* (1867), *Egyptian
Dancing Girls* (1868), and *The Grand Chamberlain of King
Sesostris the Great* (1869).

In 1870 Alma Tadema moved to London, and received
more direct Egyptian influence, for he at first rented the
house of the artist Frederick Goodall, who was travelling
in Egypt at the time. Both Frederick and his brother
Edward painted a number of scenes of people and places
in contemporary Egypt. In 1872 Alma Tadema returned to
the theme of the death of the firstborn: this later version
is larger, with much more detail, all painstakingly
researched, but it somehow lacks the poignancy of the
earlier picture. He also returned to the motif of
lamentation over a mummy, in *An Egyptian Widow*. Here
too the detail is lovingly depicted, almost to the detriment
of the true subject – the sorrowing widow crouched
beside her husband's mummified body in its cartonnage
case on a bier. Just included in the scene on the right is a
chest upon which stand the four canopic jars holding the
deceased's internal organs removed during the embalming
process. The great wooden sarcophagus, with heavy
pillars at each corner and resting on a sledge, is typical of
the Graeco-Roman period in Egypt and could have been
based on the 2nd-century A D sarcophagus of Soter,
Archon of Thebes, in the British Museum.

For all his Egyptian subjects – and there were twenty-
six major ones and some smaller pieces – Alma Tadema
did not visit Egypt until late in life, in 1902, when he
went for six weeks at the invitation of Sir John Aird to
attend the dedication of the Asyut Barrage and the Aswan
Dam. For Aird in 1904 he painted *The Finding of Moses*,
which includes a view of the Giza pyramids. Once more,
great attention is paid to detail, down to the cartouches of
Ramesses II seen on the water-pot stands.

The only other 19th-century artist who comes close to
Alma Tadema as a painter of historical pictures set in

Sir Lawrence Alma Tadema, *The Sad Father*, 1859 (Opus x)

Sir Lawrence Alma Tadema, *Pastimes in Ancient Egypt: 3,000
Years Ago*, 1863 (Opus xviii)

Sir Lawrence Alma Tadema, *An Egyptian Widow*, 1872 (Opus
xcix)

Sir Lawrence Alma Tadema, *The Finding of Moses*, 1904 (Opus CCCLXXVII)

Edwin Long, *Pharaoh's Daughter – The Finding of Moses*, 1886

Edwin Long, *Alethe, a Priestess of Isis*, 1888

Egypt is Edwin Long (1829–91). Long travelled extensively in Europe and, like David Roberts, was captivated by Spain. In 1874 he visited Egypt and Syria, and thereafter his pictures frequently had Near Eastern settings and biblical themes. His best-known picture is perhaps *The Babylonian Marriage Market*, painted in 1875. From that he went on to explore a number of Egyptian subjects, usually on a vast scale. As in other works of the time, the ancient settings gave respectability to portrayals of girls clad lightly, if at all.

Like Alma Tadema, Long was concerned with the accuracy of his background details. He had a small collection of Egyptian antiquities which he used as props, and he also copied objects in museums [II]. He would set up a combination of objects and small wax models, grouping them for the subject of his picture: a sketch by M. Renouard, exhibited at the Royal Academy in 1888, shows Long building up the setting for *The Crown of Justification*, a depiction of the ancient Egyptian custom of 'judging' the dead recorded by Diodorus Siculus, which the Academy displayed in the same year.

Most of Long's Egyptian damsels have a languid look and very similar physical characteristics. His treatment of *Pharaoh's Daughter – The Finding of Moses* (1886) makes an interesting comparison with Alma Tadema's later picture on the same theme – one a vast panorama, the other an intimate scene given local colour as much by the vegetation as by the sculpted lions and hieroglyphic inscription. Long's greatest work, literally as well as figuratively, is *Anno Domini or The Flight into Egypt*, painted in 1883 [III]. It teems with detail and is a study in contrasts, between Christian simplicity and pagan fervour, the Virgin Mary with the Christ Child and the antique Mother, Isis, with her son, Horus. The details show Long at his most scholarly, drawing upon his experience of Egypt as well as published authorities.

Long's Egyptian and Near Eastern pictures usually have specific biblical or historical associations, but he departed curiously from his custom in *Alethe, a Priestess of Isis* (1888). The young girl again has the Long languid look; she is pensively feeding sacred ibises, birds normally associated with Thoth, god of writing and wisdom, rather than Isis.

The suicide of the last queen of Egypt, Cleopatra VII, attracted many painters as a subject from the Renaissance onwards. Most saw her as the epitome of a woman scheming in any way she can, especially through sexual wiles, to achieve her ends. Makart's Cleopatra, despite her antique trappings, remains Rubensesque. Long, on the other hand, in his *Love's Labour's Lost* (1885), saw her as a young, tragic figure accepting her fate.

Like his exact contemporary Alma Tadema, Sir Edward Poynter (1836–1919) used Greece and Rome as well as

Egypt for the settings of his paintings; but unlike other historical artists he was practically concerned with the survival of the remains of ancient Egypt, serving as honorary secretary of a preservation society founded in 1889.

Poynter's *Israel in Egypt*, painted in 1867 when he was only thirty-one, is remarkable for the clarity and apparent precision of all the details in a canvas 3.12 metres (10 feet 4 inches) long, which shows the Israelites working as slaves for the Egyptians. In the foreground, a lion sculpture is being hauled along on a wheeled carriage, presumably to join its fellows in the centre background, before the second pylon of the temple – from which banners fly, a careful archaeological touch. Poynter could not have copied a scene of sculpture being moved in this way, however: ancient Egyptians did not know the wheel, and had to use rollers and levers (as Belzoni did to move the Younger Memnon [XVIII]). The lion is modelled on one of a pair in the British Museum presented by Lord Prudhoe in 1835, which are inscribed for Amenophis III of the 18th Dynasty. The temple on the right is a mixture of those at Luxor [XIV] and Edfu [57]. The obelisk is not that of Luxor but that of Heliopolis, with the cartouche of Sesostris I of the 12th Dynasty [4]. To the left of the lion is a Ptolemaic temple, in the left distance the picturesque group of buildings on the island of Philae, complete with Trajan's Kiosk [XXIV]; behind them looms the Great Pyramid of Giza, and the horizon is closed by the Theban hills [XIII].

*Israel in Egypt* shows how the approach to accurate representation and reconstruction of ancient Egypt had changed since the time of the *Description* [30, 60]. The late

Hans Makart, *The Death of Cleopatra*, 1876

Alan Sorrell, one of the best-known and most able creators of historical reconstructions, considered that Poynter's picture failed totally, because it was 'a mere conglomeration of unassimilated facts'. But Sorrell's concern was for place, the scholarly reconstruction of specific buildings and sites, whereas Poynter's was for people in history – the carefully rendered setting as an aid to the imagination, a background for human action in which the spectator is almost a participant. The descendants of Poynter's grand composition in the 20th century are not paintings, but the sets for all those epics made by Cecil B. De Mille and others in the golden age of Hollywood.

Edward John Poynter, *Israel in Egypt*, 1867

# Select Bibliography

*Some manuscript sources*

BARRY, Sir Charles – albums of drawings, plans and elevations in the Drawings Collection, British Architectural Library, Royal Institute of British Architects, London, and in the Griffith Institute, Oxford

—MS diary of travels in the Drawings Collection, RIBA, London

BELZONI, Giovanni Battista – drawings in the City Museum and Art Gallery, Bristol, and the Museo Civico, Padua

—letters in the Museo Civico, Padua, and by him and his wife Sarah in the Author's collection

BONOMI, Joseph – drawings amongst the Hay MSS in the British Library, London: *see* Hay

BURTON, James – 63 volumes of drawings in the British Library, London, Add. MSS 25613-75

CATHERWOOD, Frederick – drawings amongst the Hay MSS in the British Library: *see* Hay

CRONSTRAND, Baltzar – some 200 drawings in the National Museum, Stockholm. *See also* George *under 'Books', below*

DODWELL, Edward – drawings of antiquities in the British Library, London, Add. MSS 33958

HAWKER, Edward James – 3 volumes of drawings in the Griffith Institute, Oxford

HAY, Robert – 49 volumes of drawings (including many by other artists in his employ, e.g. Bonomi, Catherwood, Lane) in the British Library, London, Add. MSS 29812-60

—diary, Add. MSS 31054

—letters, Add. MSS 38510

HOSKINS, George Alexander – drawings in the Griffith Institute, Oxford

HUYOT, Jean Nicolas – journal and drawings in the Bibliothèque Nationale, Paris, amongst the Nestor L'Hôte papers: *see* L'Hôte

LANE, Edward William – drawings and notes in the Griffith Institute, Oxford, and the British Library, London, Add. MSS 34080–88. *See also* Ahmed *under 'Books', below*

L'HÔTE, Nestor – MSS and drawings in the Bibliothèque Nationale, Paris, Nouv. Acq. Franç. 20396, 20402, 20404, and in the Louvre, Paris, E. 25423a and b. *See also* Vandier D'Abbadie *under 'Books', below*

PARKE, Henry – architectural drawings in the Drawings Collection, RIBA, London

PRISSE D'AVENNES, A. C. T. E. – MSS and drawings in the Bibliothèque Nationale, Paris, Nouv. Acq. Franç. 20416–49

SALT, Henry – papers and drawings in the collection of Sir Michael Salt, Dorset; some negatives in the Griffith Institute, Oxford

WILKINSON, Sir John Gardner – 56 bound volumes, folders and notebooks formerly on loan to the Griffith Institute, Oxford (where negatives held), returned to the family in 1981

YOUNG, Thomas – notes on the decipherment of hieroglyphs in the British Library, London, Add. MSS 27281-85

*Books*

AHMED, L. *Edward W. Lane*, London 1978

ALDRED, C. 'The Temple of Dendur', *The Metropolitan Museum of Art Bulletin*, New York, 36, no. 1, 1978

AMPÈRE, J. J. *Voyage en Egypte et Nubie,* Paris 1868

ATHANASI, G. d' *Researches and Discoveries in Upper Egypt under the Direction of Henry Salt Esq.*, London 1836

BALLANTYNE, J. *The Life of David Roberts RA*, Edinburgh 1866

BARRY, Rev. A. *The Life and Works of Sir Charles Barry*, London 1867

BARTLETT, W. H. *The Nile Boat*, London 1850

BELZONI, G. *Narrative of the Operations and Recent Discoveries within the Pyramids, Temples, Tombs, and Excavations, in Egypt and Nubia; and of a Journey to the Coast of the Red Sea, in search of the Ancient Berenice; and another to the Oasis of Jupiter Ammon*, London 1820

— *Forty-four Plates illustrative of the Researches and Operations of Belzoni in Egypt and Nubia*, London 1820

— *Six new plates*, London 1822

BOSSI, S., and COOPER, E. J. *Views of Egypt and Nubia*, London 1822

BURCKHARDT, J. L. *Travels in Nubia*, London 1819

CAILLAUD, F. *Voyage à l'oasis de Thèbes . . . 1815–1818,* Paris 1821

CHAMPOLLION, J. F. *Lettre à M. Dacier . . .*, Paris 1822, reprinted 1922

— *Lettres écrites de l'Egypte*, Paris 1833

— *Monuments de l'Egypte et de la Nubie*, Paris 1845

CHAMPOLLION-FIGEAC, M. *L'Obélisque de Louqsor transporté à Paris*, Paris 1833

COMBES, E. *Voyage en Egypte, en Nubie*, Paris 1846

CURL, J. S. *The Egyptian Revival: An introductory study of a recurring theme in the history of taste*, London 1982

DAWSON, W. R., and UPHILL, E. P. *Who was Who in Egyptology*, 2nd rev. ed., London 1972

DE MONTULE, E. *Travels in Egypt in 1818 and 1819*, London 1823

DENON, D. V. *Voyage dans la Basse et la Haute Egypte*, Paris 1802

— *Travels in Upper and Lower Egypt* (trans. by A. Aiken), London 1803

DESCRIPTION DE L'EGYPTE *see* Panckoucke, C. L. F.

DE VERNINAC SAINT-MAUR, E. *Voyage du Luxor*, Paris 1835

DU CAMP, M. *Le Nil, Egypte et Nubie*, Paris 1852

EDWARDS, A. B. *A Thousand Miles up the Nile*, London 1877; 2nd ed. 1889

EMERY, W. B. *Egypt in Nubia*, London 1965

FLAUBERT, G. *Flaubert in Egypt* (trans. and ed. by F. Steegmuller), London 1972

FORBIN, L. N. P. A. *Voyage dans le Levant*, Paris 1819

— *Travels in Egypt 1817–1818*, London 1819

GAU, F. C. *Antiquités de la Nubie, ou Monuments inédits des bords du Nil, entre la première et la deuxième cataracte*, Paris 1824

GEORGE, B., and PETERSON, B. *Die Karnak-Zeichnungen von Baltzar Cronstrand 1836–1837*, Stockholm 1979

— *Baltzar Cronstrand I Egypten 1836–1837: En svensk officer bland faraoniska och gravar*, Stockholm 1980

GREENER, L. *The Discovery of Egypt*, London 1966

GROBERT, J. F. L. *Description des pyramindes de Ghizé . . .*, Paris 1801

GUITERMAN, H. *David Roberts R.A. 1796–1864*, London (the Author) 1978

HABACHI, L. *The Obelisks of Egypt*, London 1978

HALLS, J. J. *Henry Salt*, London 1834

HAMILTON, W. *Aegyptiaca*, London 1809

HEAD, C. F. *Eastern and Egyptian Scenery, Ruins, &c . . .*, London 1833

HEROLD, J. C. *Bonaparte in Egypt*, London 1963

IRBY, J., and MANGLES, C. *Travels in Egypt and Nubia*, London 1823

JOLLOIS, P. *Journal d'un ingénieur 1798–1802* (ed. by G. Maspero), Paris 1904

JOMARD, E. *Description de l'Egypte*, Paris n.d. [c. 1812]

— *Recueil d'observations et de mémoires sur l'Egypte . . .*, Paris n.d. [?1812]

JONES, O. *Views on the Nile*, London 1843

LEBAS, J. B. A *L' Obélisque de Luxor*, Paris 1839

LEGH, T. *Narrative of a Journey in Egypt and the country beyond the Cataracts*, London 1816

LEPSIUS, R. *Denkmäler aus Aegypten und Aethiopien*, 6 pt. in 12 vol., Berlin 1849–59

— *Discoveries in Egypt, Ethiopia, and the Peninsula of Sinai, in the years 1842–1845*, 2nd ed., London 1853

L'HÔTE, N. *L'Obélisque de Louqusor*, Paris 1836

— *Lettres de l'Egypte*, Paris 1840

LLOYD, C. *The Nile Campaign: Nelson and Napoleon in Egypt*, Newton Abbot 1973

MACQUITTY, W. *Abu Simbel*, London 1965

— *Island of Isis: Philae, Temple of the Nile*, London 1976

MANNING, S. *The Land of the Pharaohs*, London 1875

MARIETTE, A. *Voyage de la Haute-Egypte*, Paris 1878–80

MAYER, L. *Views in Egypt*, London 1804

MAYES, S. *The Great Belzoni*, London 1959

PANCKOUCKE, C. L. F. [publisher] *Description de l'Egypte ou recueil des observations et des recherches qui ont été faites en Egypte pendant l'expédition de l'armée française*, Paris 1809, 2nd ed. 1823 (24 vol.: 1–5, Antiquités descriptions; 6–10, Antiquités mémoires)

PRESCOTT, H. F. M. *Once to Sinai: The further pilgrimage of Friar Felix Fabri*, London 1957

PRISSE D'AVENNES, E. *L'Histoire de l'Art Egyptien . . .*, Paris 1858–77

QUICK, R. *The Life and Works of Edwin Long R.A.*, Bournemouth 1931, reprinted 1970

REYBAUD, L. *Histoire de l'expédition française en Egypte*, Paris 1828

RHIND, A. H. *Thebes, its Tombs and their Tenants*, London 1862

RIFAUD, J. J. *Voyages 1805–27*, Paris 1830

ROBERTS, D. *Egypt and Nubia*, 3 vol., London 1846–50 (with notes on the plates by W. Brockedon)

— *The Holy Land, . . . Egypt and Nubia*, London 1855–56 (in reduced format, with different notes by W. Brockedon)

ROSELLINI, L. *I Monumenti dell'Egitto e della Nubia*, Pisa 1832

ST JOHN, J. A. *Egypt and Nubia*, London 1845

SCHNEIDER, H. D. *Taffeh: Rond de wederopbouw van een Nubische tempel*, The Hague 1979

SCOTTISH ARTS COUNCIL *Artist Adventurer: David Roberts 1796–1864*, Edinburgh 1981 (with contributions by Helen Guiterman, *et al.*)

SEARIGHT, S. *The British in the Middle East*, London 1969, rev. ed. 1979

SWANSON, V. G. *Sir Lawrence Alma-Tadema*, London 1977

TRIGGER, B. *Nubia under the Pharaohs*, London 1976

VANDIER D'ABBADIE, J. *Nestor L'Hôte (1804–1842): choix de documents conservés à la Bibliothèque Nationale et aux archives du Musée du Louvre*, Leiden 1963

VYSE, H., and PERRING, J. S. *Operations carried on at the Pyramids of Gizeh*, 3 vol. London 1840–42

WILKINSON, J. G. *General View of Egypt*, London 1835

— *Manners and Customs of the Ancient Egyptians*, 3 vol., new ed. (rev. by Samuel Birch), London 1878

WILSON, J. A. *Signs and Wonders upon Pharaoh*, Chicago 1964

# List of Illustrations

Dimensions are given in centimetres and in inches, height before width

III Edwin Long, *Anno Domini or The Flight into Egypt*, 1883
Oil, 243.8 × 487.7 (96 × 192)
Russell-Cotes Art Gallery and Museum, Bournemouth

IV Vivant Denon, *Measuring the column of Pompey, Alexandria*, July 1798
Watercolour, 26.2 × 20.6 (10⅜ × 8 1/16)
Searight Collection, London

V James Gillray, *'L'Insurrection de l'Institut Amphibie' – The Pursuit of Knowledge*, 12 March 1799
Hand-coloured etching
Author's collection

VI Vivant Denon, *View of 'Cleopatra's Obelisk', Alexandria*, July 1798
Watercolour, 25 × 20 (9 13/16 × 7⅞)
Searight Collection, London

VII David Roberts, *The Pyramids of Geizeeh from the Nile*
Hand-coloured lithograph, from D. Roberts, *Egypt and Nubia*, London 1846–50, I

VIII David Roberts, *Pyramids of Geizeeh*
Hand-coloured lithograph, from D. Roberts, *Egypt and Nubia*, London 1846–50, II

**Illustrations on pp. 42–57**

p.42 *Portrait of Giovanni Belzoni in Turkish dress*
Lithograph by C. Hullmandel after the drawing by Maxim Gauci used as frontispiece to Belzoni's *Narrative*, London 1820

Obverse and reverse of a bronze medal commemorating the opening of the Second Pyramid (the pyramid of Chephren) at Giza by Belzoni, 2 March 1818, by T. I. Wells after William Brockedon
Diam. 5.5 (2 3/16)
Author's collection

p.43 A. Aglio, *Memorial engraving of Giovanni Belzoni*, commissioned by Sarah Belzoni, 1823
British Museum, London

p.44 *Portrait of Henry Salt*, 1834 (detail)
Engraving by C. Heath after the portrait by J. J. Halls
Author's collection

John Hayter, *Portrait of Charles Barry*, 1838
Wash heightened with white, red and brown chalk, 59 × 46 (23¼ × 18⅛)
Private collection

p.45 Maxim Gauci, *William John Bankes M.P. in oriental dress, c.* 1820 (detail)
Pencil, size of whole 36.8 × 27.5 (14½ × 10⅞)
Searight Collection, London

p.46 Henry Wyndham Phillips, *Sir John Wilkinson*, 1844
Oil

The Rosetta Stone, inscribed in honour of Ptolemy V Epiphanes (205–180 BC)
Basalt, 114 × 72 (44⅞ × 28⅜)
British Museum, London

p.47 Obverse of a bronze medallion commemorating the death of Baron Antoine Isaac Silvestre de Sacy, 1838, by Depaulis
Diam. 6.1 (2⅜)
Author's collection

*Portrait of Dr Thomas Young*, 1830 (detail)
Engraving by G. Adcock after the portrait by Sir Thomas Lawrence
Author's collection

Léon Cogniet, *Portrait of Jean François Champollion*, 1831
Oil, 73.5 × 60 (28⅞ × 23⅝)
Louvre, Paris

p.49 Obverse and reverse of a bronze medal commemorating David Roberts, 1875, by G. Morgan for the Art-Union of London
Diam. 5.7 (2¼)
Author's collection

p.50 Daguerrotype of Karl Richard Lepsius, 1850

p.51 Georg Frey, *The Prussian Expedition celebrating the birthday of King Friedrich Wilhelm IV on top of the pyramid of Cheops, 15 October 1842*
Engraving reproduced in Bernhard Lepsius, *Das Haus Lepsius*, Berlin 1933
By courtesy of Mrs Susanne Lepsius

p.53 Photograph of Amelia B. Edwards

p.54 Mrs J. Blackburn, *Discovery of a Mummy in an excavation near Thebes in the presence of H.R.H. the Prince of Wales*, 18 March 1862
From Samuel Birch, *The Papyrus of Nas-khem*, London ('Printed for private circulation by desire of H.R.H. The Prince of Wales') 1863
Author's collection

William Simpson, *Dhahabîa of the Prince and Princess of Wales on the Nile*, February 1869
Pencil and wash, 13 × 16.2 (5½ × 6½)
By courtesy of Sotheby Parke Bernet & Co.

p.55 William Simpson, *The Emperor of Austria ascending the Great Pyramid*, 24 November 1869
Watercolour, blue and grey wash with pencil, 21.7 × 27.5 (8 9/16 × 10⅞)
Searight Collection, London

Reverse of a bronze medallion commemorating the attendance of the Emperor Franz Joseph at the opening of the Suez Canal, 1869, by J. Tautenhayn
Diam. 7.1 (2 13/16)
Author's collection

p.56 Map of Egypt
Drawn by Hanni Bailey

p.57 Reverse of a bronze medal commemorating the French conquest of Lower Egypt in Year VII (1798), by L. Brenet
Diam. 3.3 (1 5/16)
Author's collection

**Plates 1–14 (pp. 58–70)**

1 Cécile, *Cleopatra's Needles and the Tower of the Romans from the south-west*, 1798
From the *Description de l'Egypte*, 2nd ed., Paris 1823, V, pl. 32

2 Luigi Mayer, *Interior view of the catacombs at Alexandria*, 1802
From L. Mayer, *Views in Egypt*, London 1804, pl. 6

3 Luigi Mayer, *An Ancient Obelisk at Matarea, formerly Heliopolis, c.* 1800
Watercolour, 18.7 × 28.7 (7⅜ × 11 9/16)
Searight Collection, London

4 William Simpson, *Heliopolis, – As it is*, 1878
Watercolour, 35 × 23.7 (13¾ × 9 5/16)
Searight Collection, London

5 Charles Barry, *Pyramids of Geeza*, 1819
Pencil, 24 × 39.8 (9 7/16 × 15⅝)
Royal Institute of British Architects, London (Barry, Pencil Sketches Egypt & Nubia, fol. 16)

6 Edward Lear, *The pyramids*, 1854
Oil
Collection of Major and Mrs Alec Wise

7 Cécile, *Two views of the Grand Gallery, Great Pyramid, Giza*, 1799
From the *Description de l'Egypte*, 2nd ed., Paris 1823, V, pl. 13

8 Luigi Mayer, *Chamber and Sarcophagus in The Great Pyramid at Gizah*
From L. Mayer, *Views in Egypt*, London 1804, pl. 19

9 Giovanni Belzoni, *Great Chamber in the Second Pyramid of Ghizeh*, 1818
From G. Belzoni, *Narrative*, London 1820

10 Edward Lane, *The Second Pyramid of Giza seen from above the top of the Great Pyramid at Giza, c.* 1826–27
Pencil sketch using *camera lucida*, 10 × 17.5 (4 × 6⅞)
British Library, London (Add. MS 34083, fol. 24)

186

40 Edward Lane, *The Horemheb colonnade, temple of Luxor*, c. 1826–27
Pencil and watercolour, 17.8 × 10 (7 × 4)
British Library, London (Add. MS 34084, fol. 20)

41 Charles Barry, *Plain of Thebes – West of the Nile*, 1819
Pencil, 28 × 48 (11 × 19)
Royal Institute of British Architects, London (Barry, Pencil Sketches Egypt and Nubia, Holy Land and Syria, fol. 4)

42 Henry Salt, *Statue of Memnon*, c. 1819
Pencil
Salt Ms. 1
By courtesy of Sir Michael Salt

**Colour plates XVI–XXII (pp. 112–21)**

XVI Ernst Weidenbach, *View of the temple of Seti I at Gourna*, 1842–44 (detail)
Hand-coloured lithograph, from R. Lepsius, *Denkmäler*, Berlin 1849–59, I

XVII William Henry Bartlett, *Memnonium*, 1845
Watercolour, 21.2 × 33 (8⅜ × 13)
Searight Collection, London

XVIII Giovanni Belzoni, *Mode in which the Younger Memnon's head (now in the British Museum) was removed by G. Belzoni*
Hand-coloured lithograph, from G. Belzoni, *Six New Plates*, London 1822

XIX David Roberts, *Entrance to the Tombs of the Kings of Thebes, Bab el Malouk* (detail)
Hand-coloured lithograph, from D. Roberts, *Egypt and Nubia*, London 1846–50, II

XX David Roberts, *Temple at Esneh, Nov. 25th 1838*
Hand-coloured lithograph, from D. Roberts, *Egypt and Nubia*, London 1846–50, I

XXI David Roberts, *The Outer Court of the Temple of Edfou, Egypt*, [1840]
Oil, 108 × 140 (43½ × 56)
Family Collection, by courtesy of Frank Bicknell Esq.

XXII David Roberts, *Kom Ombo, Nov. 21st 1838*
Hand-coloured lithograph, from D. Roberts, *Egypt and Nubia*, London 1846–50, I

**Plates 43–66 (pp. 122–51)**

43 Charles Barry, *Memnonium, Upper Egypt*, 1819
Pencil, 29.8 × 48.6 (11¾ × 19⅛)
Royal Institute of British Architects, London (Barry, Pencil Sketches Egypt & Nubia, fol. 22)

44 Captain Charles Francklin Head, *Part of the interior of the temple of Medinah Habou*, January 1830
Watercolour and sepia wash, 27.5 × 40.6 (10¹³⁄₁₆ × 16)
Searight Collection, London

45 Charles Barry, *Supposed palace, Medinet Abou*, 1819
Pencil, 25.5 × 39.6 (10¹⁄₁₆ × 15⅝)
Royal Institute of British Architects, London (Barry, Pencil Sketches Egypt & Nubia, fol. 23)

46 Giovanni Belzoni, *Topographical Map of the Valley of Biban Ell Malook, in which the Tombs of the Kings are situated*, 1817
From G. Belzoni, *Narrative*, London 1820

47 Captain Charles Francklin Head, *Approach to the tombs of the kings at Thebes, Biban-el-Muluk*, January 1830
Watercolour and sepia wash, 24.3 × 40 (9⁹⁄₁₆ × 15¾)
Searight Collection, London

48 Owen Jones, *Interior of the tomb of Ramesses V [IX]*, 1832–33
From O. Jones, *Views on the Nile*, London 1843

49 Vivant Denon, *Tombs of the nobles at Thebes*, 1798
From V. Denon, *Voyage*, Paris 1802, pl. XLII

50 Dutertre, *The Temple of Armant (Hermonthis) from the west*, 1798
From the *Description de l'Egypte*, 2nd ed., Paris 1823, II, pl. 92

51 Edward Hawker, *Ermenth or Hermonthis*, 5 February 1851
Wash, 25.4 × 17.5 (10 × 6¾)
Griffith Institute, Ashmolean Museum, Oxford (Hawker MS I, fol. 18)

52 Amelia B. Edwards, *Temple of Esneh*, 1874
From A. B. Edwards, *A Thousand Miles up the Nile*, 2nd ed., London 1889, p. 161

53 J. Jollois and R. E. Devilliers du Terrage, *Reconstruction of the interior of the portico of the temple of Esna (Latopolis) with a religious procession*, 1798
From the *Description de l'Egypte*, 2nd ed., Paris 1823, I, pl. 83

54 Cécile, *Interior of a large tomb at El Kab*, 1798
From the *Description de l'Egypte*, 2nd ed., Paris 1823, I, pl. 67

55 George Alexander Hoskins, *Small shrine of Amenophis III, El Kab*, 1832–33
Wash, 22.4 × 14.3 (8¹³⁄₁₆ × 5⅝)

Griffith Institute, Ashmolean Museum, Oxford (Hoskins MS II, fol. 115)

56 Dutertre, *The temple of El Kab*, 1798
From the *Description de l'Egypte*, 2nd ed., Paris 1823, I, pl. 66

57 David Roberts, *Edfu*, 23 November 1838
Watercolour, 32.3 × 48.2 (12¾ × 19)
The Pierpont Morgan Library, New York

58 Vivant Denon, *The temple of Edfu*, 1798
From V. Denon, *Voyage*, Paris 1802

59 Balzac, *Rock-cut stelae at the landing place of the Silsileh quarries*, 1798
From the *Description de l'Egypte*, 2nd ed., Paris 1823, I, pl. 47

60 J. Jollois and R. E. Devilliers du Terrage, *Reconstruction view of the double temple at Kom Ombo with the entrance pylon on the right and mamisi on the left*, 1798
From the *Description de l'Egypte*, 2nd ed., Paris 1823, I, pl. 46

61 Charles Barry, *Koum Ombos*, 1819
Pencil, 27.7 × 45.3 (10⅞ × 17⅞)
Royal Institute of British Architects, London (Barry, Pencil Sketches Egypt & Nubia, fol. 28)

62 Edward Lear, *Assouan, 7–8 a.m., 9 February 1854* (detail)
Watercolour, size of whole 32.4 × 47 (12¾ × 18½)
University of Liverpool Fine Art Collections

63 Vivant Denon, *Quarries at Aswan*, 1798
From V. Denon, *Voyage*, Paris 1802, pl. LXVIII

64 Charles Barry, *Temple in the island of Elephantina near the first Cataracts. Upper Egypt*, 1818
Pencil, 19.9 × 27.7 (7¹³⁄₁₆ × 10¹⁵⁄₁₆)
Royal Institute of British Architects, London (Barry, Pencil Sketches Egypt & Nubia, fol. 33)

p.149 Obverse of a bronze medallion commemorating the international rescue of the monuments of Abu Simbel, 1965–68, by E. Monti
Diam. 6 (2⁵⁄₁₆)
Author's collection

65 Edward William Cooke, *Philae, Nubia*, 21 December 1874
Pencil and grey wash, 11.8 × 20.6 (4¾ × 8¼)
Searight Collection, London

66 L.M.A. Linant de Bellefonds, *Great Temple of Isis, Philae, seen from the southern tip of the island*
Watercolour, 33.8 × 50 (13¼ × 19⅝)
Searight Collection, London

187

# Index

# Acknowledgments for Photographs

The author and publishers are grateful
to the individuals and institutions
mentioned in the List of Illustrations.
Photographs for the figures (referred to
in *italic* type) and for the black-and-
white and colour plates are also due to
the following:

Peter Clayton: *pages 7, 11, 12, 15,
17–19, 24, 25 left and centre, 26, 29, 30
right, 31, 42–44, 47 left above and below,*
*49, 54 above, 55 below, 57, 71, 149;*
plates 9, 11, 13, 25, 39, 46, 52, 73, V,
XVIII, XXVIII, XXIX—DSB Photographic
Services Ltd, Glasgow: plate XXI—
Michael Meyersfield, Johannesburg:
*page 179 above*—Philip Barker, London:
*pages 25 right, 45, 55 above, 177 below;*
plates 2–4, 8, 14, 21, 38, 44, 47, 48,
65–67, 74, 76, 78, IV, VI, XVII, XXIII,
XXX—Egypt Exploration Society,
London: *page 53*—Fotomas, London:
plates I, VII, X, XI, XIV, XIX, XX, XXII—

John R. Freeman, London: *pages 20–22;*
plates 1, 7, 12, 16–20, 22, 24, 26–28,
30–32, 34, 36, 49, 50, 53, 54, 56, 58–60,
63, 68, VIII, IX, XII, XIII, XV, XVI,
XXIV–XXVII—Sotheby Parke Bernet &
Co., London: *page 180 above*—Eileen
Tweedy, London: *page 51*—Griffith
Institute, Ashmolean Museum, Oxford:
*page 46 above;* plates 42, 69—Bulloz,
Paris: *page 16*—Giraudon, Paris: *page 47
right*—Harold Morris, Wimborne: *page
180 below.*